NEW DIRECTIONS FOR HIGHER EDUCATION

Martin Kramer, *University of California, Berkeley*
EDITOR-IN-CHIEF

Managing Change in Higher Education

Douglas W. Steeples
Aurora University

EDITOR

Number 71, Fall 1990

JOSSEY-BASS INC., PUBLISHERS
San Francisco • Oxford

MANAGING CHANGE IN HIGHER EDUCATION
Douglas W. Steeples (ed.)
New Directions for Higher Education, no. 71
Volume XVIII, number 2
Martin Kramer, Editor-in-Chief

LC 85-644752   ISSN 0271-0560   ISBN 1-55542-807-X

NEW DIRECTIONS FOR HIGHER EDUCATION is part of The Jossey-Bass
Higher Education Series and is published quarterly by Jossey-Bass Inc.,
Publishers (publication number USPS 990-880). Second-class postage
paid at San Francisco, California, and at additional mailing offices. Post-
master: Send address changes to Jossey-Bass Inc., Publishers, 350 San-
some Street, San Francisco, California 94104.

EDITORIAL CORRESPONDENCE should be sent to the Editor-in-Chief,
Martin Kramer, 2807 Shasta Road, Berkeley, California 94708.

Cover photograph and random dot
by Richard Blair/Color & Light © 1990.

Printed on acid-free paper in the United States of America.

CONTENTS

EDITOR'S NOTES

I keep in my office a poster that occasionally provides some comic relief in the midst of academic problems and responsibilities. It features a close-up photograph of hundreds of white turkeys, shown from the shoulders up, standing densely packed, with characteristically vacant faces. Beneath the picture is a caption in several languages, reading, "Now that we are organized, what do we do?" The photograph and caption offer a metaphor for American higher education just now, for, in many respects, our colleges and universities are like the turkeys in the poster: They are numerous (some would say too numerous), they stand shoulder to shoulder (at least as to the major elements of the mission of higher education), and they are often unsure how to meet the daunting new challenges confronting them in an era of pervasive change. Responding to these challenges, determining "what we do," is the key task of higher education administrators during the closing years of the twentieth century.

The nature of this key task is the subject of this volume. A few years ago, a university chief business officer and former president of the National Association of College and University Business Officers, looking back on a rich career and forward to retirement, liked to quip that he was not sure whether he had learned many new things across the years or just the same thing thirty-five times. He knew better. In the span of his career he had dealt with the post–World War II explosion in enrollments that transformed higher education. During that expansive epoch, which lasted into the 1970s, colleges and universities were a major growth industry. Public policy, meanwhile, supported expansion, providing liberal funding for financial aid for students, for appropriations for construction and renovation of facilities, for expenditures for new equipment, for contracts for research, and more. Then, suddenly (it seemed to some), higher education came of age, in a sharply altered environment. Campuses across the country, like it or not, had to contend with profound changes.

Describing our own era, one recent writer commented that "the era of growth is past, and the postwar assumptions about the nation are no longer accurate" (Levine and Associates, 1989, p. xi). In entire regions of the United States there is and will continue to be for at least the remainder of the century a shrinkage of the population of eighteen- to twenty-two-year-olds from which colleges and universities have traditionally recruited most of their students. Many of the areas of greatest loss in this population harbor what is now coming to seem to be an unnecessarily large number of institutions of higher learning, with the capacity (and fiscal need) to serve far more students than may be available to them. Meanwhile, public policy has come to emphasize new priorities, resulting in a diversion of appropriations away from higher education. The formerly genteel admissions game, which for years emphasized processing applications for enrollment, has become hotly competitive and oriented toward aggressive marketing. At the same time, the rapid growth of minority populations portends a sea change in national demography. In the emerging balance of things, those colleges and universities that have not already engaged aggressively in affirmative action recruiting will find it necessary now to attract and serve ethnic and racial minority students in order to maintain enrollments and financial stability.

Early in this century, economist Thorstein Veblen ([1918] 1957) scathingly criticized the triumph of the corporate model in higher education, with its expanding bureaucracies and corps of professional managers and presidents, the "captains of erudition" who were the exact equivalents of the rapacious heads of giant businesses (p. 65). This development, through which business values displaced academic values, was for Veblen a betrayal of the proper mission of academia. Today, we can, while maintaining a properly critical stance, find reasons to be grateful for the maturation of our academic institutions. Higher education is better organized than ever before, and it is clear that this high level of organization is necessary to meet the demands of the times. Even small colleges are complex organizations with impressive physical plants, curricula composed of hundreds of courses, and a need for a wide array of management functions. If the choice is between assigning management to professional administrators or requiring professors to secure their own chalk and other supplies, arrange for the maintenance of the campus, manage institutional resources and maintain records, and adapt their institutions to a highly volatile environment, it is hard to doubt the wisdom of our current administrative arrangements and the organization of higher education of which they are an integral part.

Thus, higher education, to return to the metaphor symbolized by my poster, is organized; recent history now dictates "what we do": We must grapple with change in order to ensure the prosperity and relevance of our colleges and universities. We administrators know this. Commonly, we view ourselves much more as change agents than as custodians. Whether responding to pressures emanating from the external environment or initiating new developments on our own, we understand that the achievement of desired change requires *management*. Managing change is the means of coping with the new conditions and challenges currently confronting academia. Managing change is the subject of this volume.

The contributors are all accomplished change agents. They have written thematic chapters addressing strategies for change and offering practical guidelines for accomplishing innovation across the range of college and university activities. The focus is on practice, not theory or research. The authors write from direct experience, providing case examples. Readers who wish further information will know whom to contact and the experience of which campuses to consult.

The opening chapter, by D. W. Farmer, provides a conceptual introduction to our subject and treats the question of strategies for change. Farmer explores the roles of the "corporate culture" of a campus, of leadership, of planning, and of process in the creation of a climate open to innovation, referring to his successful experience at King's College in Wilkes-Barre, Pennsylvania. He closes with a consideration of ways to implement and sustain change, once it has been agreed on.

James B. Kashner, in Chapter Two, explores at length the nature of the corporate culture of higher education at large and of particular institutions. After reviewing the roles of cherished values and traditional assumptions, he considers the influence of formally defined organizational structure and of the roles and statuses of individuals on a campus. He concludes with recommendations, many of them arising from accomplishments at College of the Southwest in Hobbs, New Mexico, of ways both to use sympathetic elements within a campus culture and to change a campus culture so as to render it more open to innovation. Alterations of the campus culture, Kashner observes, must often be secured *before* any other major desired changes can win approval and be implemented.

Charles A. Dominick, in Chapter Three, shows how the revision of the mission statement of Wittenberg University in Springfield, Ohio, can stand as a model for similar efforts on other campuses. Wittenberg's success depended on a number of crucial elements, including strong presidential leadership, a broadly participatory process that encouraged the achievement of consensus, an appropriate reliance on research, and provision of adequate support for the task. The resulting mission statement reminds us that any suitable such document must strike a balance between elements in an institution's heritage and elements common to all mission statements, yielding, in the end, a mix peculiar to one campus.

In Chapter Four, Keith W. Mathews shows how strategic changes in the allocation of financial resources may enable a college or university to respond to pressures or opportunities from without or to undertake or sustain initiatives on its own. Ohio Wesleyan University, confronted with a dramatic enrollment decline, furnishes an example of an institution that reallocated resources to improve its fortunes. It employed such devices as cost cutting, the expenditure of accumulated reserves, and program innovations that garnered new support to combat its problems successfully. Baldwin-Wallace College, through planning, goal setting, careful determination of budgeting priorities, and admissions activities, deployed fiscal resources so as to maintain a desired program of institutional growth. The experiences of both of these institutions illustrate how effective a considered use of financial resources can be for administrators faced with the need to make changes.

Richard J. Wood follows, in Chapter Five, with a discussion of approaches to changing what is often the most intractable component of academic institutions: the educational program. Describing his work at Earlham College in Indiana, he stresses the entrepreneurial dimensions of presidential leadership as the means of encouraging increased program coherence. Referring to earlier work as chief academic officer at Whittier College in California, he explains the process used there to create agreement about institutional mission and the resulting need to revise the general education program.

James L. Pence continues, in Chapter Six, with an incisive commentary on the pivotal importance of college and university academic personnel policies and faculty handbooks, and he offers a detailed road map for adapting them. He draws on experience as a consultant for handbook and policy revision at several institutions and on lessons learned during a successful two-year revision effort at the University of Southern Colorado. He recommends an approach that conceives of handbooks in terms of a literary metaphor—regarding them as vehicles for relating the institutional saga—and that can open the way for institutional changes far beyond the realm of faculty personnel policies.

In Chapter Seven, Helmut Hofmann summarizes ways to cultivate new sources of external funding for colleges and universities. He emphasizes the importance of thorough preparation, careful staff selection and development, patient cultivation, realistic budgeting, and appropriate personal contacts in securing support from new contributors. His practical advice rests on experience as a college president and as chief officer of the Western Independent Colleges Fund.

Craig A. Green, in Chapter Eight, describes techniques for recruiting students from new sources. Green uses Westminster College of Salt Lake City for illustration. He stresses the importance of a knowledge of marketing, market research, sound organization, scholarship and financial aid policy, shifts in promotional approaches, and changes in academic offerings as elements in a strong recruiting program.

In Chapter Nine, George N. Rainsford turns to a more specific problem in student recruitment. He offers the experience of Lynchburg College, Virginia, as an example of how colleges and universities can reply positively to the emerging demography of America, attracting and adequately serving student bodies that contain representative numbers from racial, ethnic, and other minority groups. Rainsford's remarks contain important advice for administrators attuned to the changing character of the population of our country.

The final chapter provides concluding observations about the business of managing change in colleges and universities. These observations highlight the considerations and problems that typically confront officers who wish to innovate and identify the threads common to successful efforts to achieve desired changes. Closing remarks emphasize the importance of directing change as a means of preserving the vitality of institutions of higher education.

Douglas W. Steeples
Editor

References

Levine, A., and Associates. *Shaping Higher Education's Future: Demographic Realities and Opportunities, 1990–2000.* San Francisco: Jossey-Bass, 1989.

Veblen, T. *The Higher Learning in America: A Memorandum on the Conduct of Universities by Businessmen.* New York: Sagamore Press, 1957. (Originally published 1918.)

Douglas W. Steeples is vice-president for academic affairs at Aurora University, Aurora, Illinois.

The ability to understand and respond to the human dimension of change is ultimately the determining factor in implementing and sustaining successful change.

Strategies for Change

D. W. Farmer

Change always carries with it a sense of violation. It thus invites resistance. Many managers in higher education are not prepared to deal with this resistance because they do not understand the nature of change and its human dimensions. Most people respond to change or its prospect with anxiety. Social organizations are by their nature conservative and protective. Social structures have been created to guard against disturbing changes. Resistance to change is particularly intense in higher education because faculty members are instinctively hyperconservative about educational matters.

The challenge for higher education today is to employ to good purpose the conservative instinct to preserve what is most valuable in its tradition, while at the same time introducing the changes required by a dynamic society entering the twenty-first century. Changing and adapting are two essential requirements for survival and growth. Internal and external pressures for change in higher education today make it more realistic for colleges and universities to ask *which* changes they must make, rather than whether or not changes will be required.

All innovations introduced in a college or university should assist in translating its strategic vision into reality. Meaningful change is much more than merely cosmetic; it is tantamount to renewal. It involves redefining values and transforming the culture of an organization. Behavioral change must follow to sustain the organizational changes introduced. Academic managers need to understand that knowledge, skills, and abilities can be learned and developed to help them implement meaningful change successfully.

NEW DIRECTIONS FOR HIGHER EDUCATION, no. 71, Fall 1990 ©Jossey-Bass Inc., Publishers

Organizational Culture

Organizational culture has recently emerged as an important field of study. An organization's culture consists of the assumptions, beliefs, and feelings that its members share. This culture finds expression in what is done, how it is done, and who is involved in doing it. It shapes decisions, actions, and communication on both an operational and a symbolic level. Failure to understand the way in which an organization's culture will interact with various contemplated change strategies thus may mean the failure of the strategies themselves.

Since members of an organization usually take its culture for granted, the culture often gains explicit recognition only after actions have transgressed its bounds and generated conflicts. Only when administrators possess a "full, nuanced understanding of the organization's culture" can they communicate effectively with its different constituencies and cultivate their support, thereby implementing decisions effectively (Tierney, 1988, p. 5).

The effective leader understands that much of the resistance to an innovation usually arises more as a result of a perceived threat to the organization's culture than as a reaction to the substance of the change. She or he knows that it is necessary to devise a strategy for change that does not appear to threaten the assumptions, values, feelings, and ways of working that the organization's members share. It is vitally important to know the culture specific to the institution in which one is working and to recognize that what will work in one organization may not work in another.

Roles of the Change Agent

Higher education generally "operates with no great sense of urgency or uncertainty—or discomfort" (Seymore, 1988, p. iv). Inertia reigns, buttressing tradition and the status quo. Thus, an agent is essential to effect any change.

A change agent may be from within or without, an individual or a team. In all cases, though, the change agent who succeeds understands the organization—its culture, its resources, and its politics. And the successful change agent plays one or more of several principal roles: catalyst, solution giver, process helper, resource linker, and confidence builder.

Catalyst. As catalyst, the change agent may help others to understand the need for change, as well as win support for a specific innovation. Often the catalyst, faced with organizational inertia, complacency, and self-satisfaction, must raise the levels of both dissatisfaction and of awareness within an institution in order to get things started. He or she must be sensitive to process; above all, the catalyst must cultivate a sense of timing so as to be able to introduce change at the most opportune moment.

Solution Giver. The role of solution giver involves both defining the substance of a needed new measure and offering specific implementation strategies. The manager, however, needs to know more than this to be successful. She or he must also know how to communicate both the solution and the ways to adapt it to the needs of a particular institution.

Process Helper. As process helper, the change agent assists others in conceptualizing and devising a strategy for successful innovation. Since most people are not skilled at setting new courses, this role extends to introducing to members of a organization specific techniques for setting objectives, diagnosing problems, identifying various possible solutions, and tailoring them to a specific corporate culture.

Resource Linker. The resource-linking role involves constructing within an organization a network of resources that will advance the intended change by bringing people, ideas, and finances together. The resources that are joined may come from outside as well as inside the institution. Highly developed communication and relationship-building skills are vital to successful efforts at linking resources.

Confidence Builder. Confidence building is a key task in sustaining change. It is needed to overcome the fear and anxiety that the prospect of change stirs in many people. It replaces these negative feelings with a sense of stability and of possibility that nourishes the capacity for self-renewal among those whose efforts are critical to sustain change. Confidence building works in tandem with the other roles that the change agent must perform.

Supportive Environment

Institutional cultures are capable of change, but leadership is required to form and transform an institution. Leadership encompasses the abilities to discern a need for change and to make it happen by creating a supportive environment.

Internal Environment. The external factors bearing on colleges and universities are well known. The environment within an institution is equally important in any discussion of change. There are internal environments that foster change, and there are those that do not. Developing openness to innovation may be difficult, but it is possible. Indeed, it is imperative if change agents are to succeed. Those who wish to create an internal environment supportive of innovation must hold one essential principle in mind:

People Make Changes. Organizations do not make changes; people do. People influence the behavior of an organization through their actions, which express the organization's culture. Developed through common experiences shared over time, this culture either supports or, more probably, opposes innovation.

If the culture resists change, the change agent's task is to transform it into one supportive of change. Introducing and maintaining over an extended period of time new shared experiences that cultivate assumptions and beliefs receptive to desired change are important steps in transforming a culture. Raising to positions of influence people within the organization who are innovators is another. Yet another is providing leadership that rewards new ideas, risk taking, cooperation, and a healthy competitive spirit.

Three Conditions Essential for Change

Many factors shape a campus culture. Three must be present if efforts to innovate are to succeed. Successful efforts to create them at King's College in Wilkes-Barre, Pennsylvania, assisted me greatly in developing a college environment where the desired change could occur.

Condition of Trust. A condition of trust is the first prerequisite for creating on a college campus a positive attitude toward change. Building trust is a slow process and one that requires mutual respect between faculty members and administrators. These two groups need to see themselves as partners in higher education, not as adversaries. Trust building must be given high priority as a consciously pursued institutional goal. Trust is not simply the result of rhetoric; it grows out of deeds. Actions define interpersonal relationships and associated expectations.

Free and open communication between faculty members and administrators is the first precondition for achieving trust. Making decisions in a way that reflects a clear and sensitive understanding of the culture of a campus also contributes to building trust. Such an understanding gives a change agent insight of critical value in choosing the most appropriate solution to a problem. It is especially crucial when the agent is designing specific change strategies, since the same goal can usually be reached through a variety of routes. Some of these will inevitably offend basic assumptions and beliefs of the organization and stir opposition to a desired change. Others will build on the campus culture while they also support change. It is important to know, in advance, which are which.

I have directed at King's College the conceptualization and implementation of an outcomes-oriented curriculum complemented by a course-embedded assessment model. This comprehensive change included a move from teacher-centered to student-centered teaching strategies in order to encourage students to become active, rather than passive, learners. The King's College culture had always assigned a high priority to teaching and student learning. Rather than approaching assessment as a means of measuring student learning in order to satisfy outside bureaucratic authorities—an approach that would have offended the institutional culture—I chose to focus on the potential benefit to students of making assessment an integral part of teaching and learning. Thus, the change could be perceived as supporting one of the central values of the existing institutional culture.

The focal point for this change was the question, "How do we use desired learning outcomes and assessment strategies to increase both the quality and quantity of student learning?"

Although many faculty members were initially opposed to this approach to educating students, they recognized the sincerity of the proposed effort to improve student learning. They also perceived the importance of being able to articulate more clearly what it means to be a teaching faculty, the idea of which is at the core of the King's College culture. Recognition of the great potential of the proposed academic innovation for strengthening the institutional culture, rather than undermining it, contributed to building trust—and thus tolerance for—the change agent.

Committed Leadership. The quality of leadership also helps fashion an institutional environment that is hospitable to change. A strong commitment from top campus leadership is indispensable; without it, change will simply not occur. It is the responsibility of top leadership to encourage innovation and to make it clear that it fully supports institutional change agents. The president and other top officers must provide consistent, obvious support for innovation and must establish a campuswide expectation that change will occur.

The president of King's College demonstrated just such leadership. He challenged the faculty to abandon a curriculum based on distribution requirements that had degenerated into a smorgasbord of unrelated course offerings and to build a curriculum possessing far greater coherence and integrity. Presidential comments, in annual addresses to the faculty, on progress or lack of progress toward the goal gave further evidence of consistent leadership. Presidential support for change significantly strengthened my role as a change agent.

As academic vice-president, I actively coached faculty members in constructing an outcomes-oriented curriculum that incorporated a course-embedded assessment model, presenting both specific suggestions as to substance and ideas as to strategy. I also participated as a colleague in a variety of faculty development programs designed to prepare faculty members to introduce student-centered learning strategies into their classrooms and to hold students responsible for transferring liberal arts learning skills into subject matter courses in all disciplines throughout all four years of undergraduate study. I also engaged in deliberate role modeling by designing and teaching a new course incorporating student-centered teaching methods and course-embedded assessment measures. Most faculty members viewed my willingness to spend time on the task and to participate in a shared faculty experience as an example of leadership that affirmed the centrality of teaching and student learning in the King's College culture. I also never allowed those who opposed the desired change to appropriate for themselves either the basic issue of academic standards or the goal of academic excellence.

Effective Planning. Effective planning can also contribute to the creation of an environment supportive of change if the learning that takes place during the planning process is seen as more valuable than the plan itself. Planning may be used as a heuristic device for introducing planned change. Planning anticipates change and an improved future. The planning process provides an opportunity for the leadership to articulate a vision for the institution. An open planning process provides the dynamics through which the vision is translated into specific planning objectives and implementation strategies. Through the planning process, the assumptions underlying the vision and its implementation become internalized in the thinking, feelings, and behavior of members of the institution, as leaders from time to time send signals as to what is most important. Planning thus bridges the vision and the desired reality; it is the essential connection.

Effective strategic planning accompanied by strategic thinking has played a key role in King's College's successful effort to make and carry out its commitment to create its future. Three factors lead in accounting for the success of the college's planning model. The first is the scheduling of much of the planning prior to the budgeting activities, in order to make clear early on what ought to be the college's agenda. The second is the development of institutional research and environmental scanning programs on which to base planning. The third is the employment of the strategic mode of thinking, which encourages the college to make decisions in the present that position it to act on opportunities envisioned in the future.

The prominent place of oral communication in planning at King's College also warrants mention here. Extensive face-to-face deliberation provides opportunities for immediate feedback, both verbal and nonverbal, on proposed objectives and strategies. Sensitivity to nonverbal feedback is invaluable for discerning the feelings of participants. It permits one to know whether or not what has been presented has been understood, has generated anxiety, or has struck a responsive chord. The ability to deal immediately with these responses, acknowledging the ideas and the feelings of people involved in the planning process, helps to nourish a widened sense of ownership and also to transform discussion of planning objectives into productive talk about implementation strategies.

Specific Implementation Strategies

Once an organizational climate supportive of innovation has been created, the change agent must turn to the identification of specific implementation strategies. The strategies selected must at once reduce resistance to and widen support for change.

The effective change agent understands the variety of possible reasons for opposition to change and employs this knowledge to obtain willing cooperation from individuals whom the change affects. The full benefit of innovation is not realized until the entire campus community accepts it with at least a modicum of enthusiasm.

Resistance occurs at the implementation stage for several reasons. Implementation maximizes disequilibrium and thus the potential for conflict. As change becomes reality, latent hostility and feelings of loss of power begin to surface. Likewise, unforeseen short-run negative consequences of the innovation become apparent. Passive resistance also poses problems, as members of the organization balk at following management's directives, refuse to apply the innovation properly, or act so as to prevent the full realization of the benefits that the change promises.

Implementation of a change, because of its feared impact on existing social relationships on a campus, challenges the need for stability. It threatens to alter the hierarchies of power and of personal prestige or status. It also prompts opposition arising from such things as inaccurate perceptions of the intended change, low tolerance for novelty on the part of persons hesitant to take risks, reluctance to admit weakness, uncertainty that the new will be better than the familiar, and genuine disagreement with the substance of the new course being embarked on.

Since no single technique for dealing with resistance to change can be used in all situations, it is important to know that a variety of techniques exists. These techniques are often more effective when used in combination than when used in isolation. As a change agent at King's College, I have used a variety of strategies to overcome opposition to change.

Participation. A participatory process is an important means of generating support for change. It is essential for innovators to recognize the human dimension of change—to recognize that it is people who make changes, sustain changes, and determine the quality of change. If those who will be affected by an intended change are able to participate in its planning and implementation, their commitment to its success tends to increase.

It is vital to monitor and to respond to feedback throughout the entire change process. Resistance will be reduced if the project is open to revision when experience so recommends. Resistance will be further reduced if change agents are able to empathize with those opposing change and thus to recognize valid objections and to relieve anxieties. If the change agent is able to discover which values of the organization the resistance represents, the agent can select specific change strategies that support rather than conflict with them.

I have found the use of a modified matrix model, characterized by cross-organizational project teams, to be the most successful mechanism for encouraging broad participation at King's College. A team is a group of doers who plan and implement their own agenda, as opposed to a committee that writes a report calling for someone else to do something. The project team in a matrix model crosses traditional organizational lines and is a vehicle for breaking down departmental and disciplinary boundaries among faculty members. Using project teams widens participation in institutional change by encouraging faculty members and administrators to look beyond narrow departmental habits of thought and to examine a variety of perspectives. Cross-organization project teams have been especially useful in implementing changes in curriculum and assessment at King's College. They have supplanted a climate that depended on departmental meetings and that tended to be political with one that tends to be more academic and more hospitable to ideas for improving curriculum, teaching, and student learning. Since the project teams are both task- and process-oriented, they require and cultivate an institutional climate characterized by cooperation rather than by competition and conflict.

Education. Reliance on formal authority to overcome resistance to change tends to be self-defeating. It may intensify feelings of hostility and opposition. This is a special danger in higher education, where faculty members value their autonomy highly. Recourse to authority may also provoke camouflaged resistance. The use of manipulative strategies can be even more problematic, since they can destroy the all-important atmosphere of trust.

The learning style of most people engaged in higher education makes them receptive to the use of information in making decisions. As a result, they require information in order to understand any proposed change. Time for investigation, questions, dialogue, reflection, application—in other words, for education—is essential for faculty members.

I believe that self-discovery is the most effective form of education. Rather than telling the faculty that the existing curriculum lacked integrity and coherence, I encouraged the faculty to study the effectiveness of the curriculum, of teaching, and of student learning at King's College. Over a period of several years, three such faculty study groups worked and arrived at similar conclusions that pointed to a need for change. The reports that resulted served to stir dissatisfaction with the status quo and to raise faculty consciousness about curricular, teaching, and learning issues. The effect was to improve greatly the prospects for change, since those whom the change would affect now recognized the need for it.

Incremental Change. The introduction of change with haste and urgency often results in error. In such a climate, action may occur before various possible implementation strategies have been thoroughly examined. Besides, in an enterprise as complex as education, it is rarely possible to implement all of the components of a desired innovation simultaneously. An incremental approach usually works best. Breaking a large change into a series of discrete smaller steps that occur sequentially over time is a powerful strategy for reducing resistance to innovation. This approach reduces the perceived magnitude of projected measures and thus the fears and uncertainty that accompany a move from the known to the unknown. Because incremental change is less threatening than global change, it provokes less resistance and holds out the prospect of greater organizational stability.

Pilot testing of desired innovations has been highly effective in overcoming much of the resistance to comprehensive new measures at King's College. This approach permits demonstration of the feasibility of intended actions before moving from one to another in a logical, incremental sequence. Pilot tests also seem tentative in that they do not require faculty members to abandon established practice forcefully and abruptly.

Preparation. Higher education offers numerous examples of unsuccessful attempts to implement change. Premature action has been one principal source of failure. Successful planned change requires more than wishing. Careful preparation is essential. The development of faculty self-confidence is imperative. Academic leaders should never ask faculty members to carry out an innovation that the latter believe they are unprepared professionally to bring to fruition. It is frequently necessary to slow the pace of change in order to gain the time required to prepare for successful implementation.

Directed and focused faculty development activity has been a significant means of preparing faculty members at King's College to implement academic innovation successfully. Faculty members want to be adequately prepared. They do not want to experience professional embarrassment. Administrators who assign a high priority to relevant faculty development measures demonstrate their support for innovation.

The words *directed* and *focused* indicate the need for clear objectives for faculty development projects. Group training in computer literacy, critical thinking, writing across the curriculum, or student-centered teaching strategies are examples of the kind of training needed for faculty members who will share in implementing an outcomes-oriented curriculum. Faculty growth plans are an effective means of connecting an individual faculty member's objectives to institutional objectives. We used faculty growth plans at King's College to encourage professors to take risks by experimenting with new student-centered teaching and learning approaches.

Incentives. Many change agents underestimate the motivational energy needed to accomplish change. Provision of incentives is particularly useful in attracting faculty support for innovation. Anything that the potential resister values may be used as an incentive. More common incentives are provision of temporary or permanent salary increases, stipends, fringe benefits, better schedules, improved working conditions, time off, and so on. The effective change agent, recognizing that individuals respond to different stimuli, will offer highly individualized incentives.

I have employed incentives to advantage at King's College as a means of initially involving faculty members in a variety of innovative efforts. Incentives have affirmed the importance of projects and the commitment of institutional leadership to them. Even the communication to professors of the sincere judgment that they possess the ability to bring about a particular change may serve as a potent mover.

Critical Mass. Many attempts at innovation in higher education have failed because change agents have invested too much energy in efforts to win support from a majority, rather than from a critical mass. The critical mass consists of the faculty leaders and opinion makers who can elicit either the support or the tolerance of their peers. Change agents must win over key faculty leaders and opinion makers *before* attempting publicly to initiate new undertakings.

Every organization contains opinion leaders, influential people whom most of their colleagues regard highly. The approval of these people is essential for an initiative to succeed. These individuals listen to and observe both the innovators and the resisters. They weigh the probable effectiveness of the proposed measure, and they assess the intensity of criticism in order to gauge the social risks associated with embracing it. It is this group who must be converted; once they are, they will encourage majority faculty support, or at least tolerance, for a proposed change.

Cultivation of the critical mass has been an especially useful element in King's College's successful efforts to change. As a change agent, I have helped faculty leaders to understand the potential academic benefits that could accrue to students who experienced a curriculum that was oriented toward student learning outcomes and that integrated assessment into the teaching and learning processes. I have employed a variety of devices to heighten faculty awareness of the need for change and to involve leaders actively early in the change process. These devices have included one-on-one discussions, involvement in faculty development programs, participation in pilot projects, and use of opinion shapers as project team leaders.

The Process of Sustaining Change

Many innovations are short-lived. Too often, change agents focus too much on implementing change and too little on sustaining it. Just as incentives help to win support for new measures, continued rewards help to sustain them. Colleges and universities should ensure that their reward systems affirm the behaviors needed both to implement and to sustain change. Contradictory reward systems sap the psychic energy that is vital for maintaining support for innovations after their enactment.

At King's College, I attended to the need to be clear about the criteria for allocating rewards and status. Faculty members who took leading roles in making changes in curriculum, assessment, and student-centered teaching became the chief beneficiaries of external funding awarded to the college; they received courseload reductions, summer stipends for further work in curriculum development, and support to attend a variety of national conferences and workshops. They were also encouraged to present their work at professional meetings and to prepare journal articles on strategies to improve both the quality and the quantity of student learning in their disciplines. In all cases, faculty experimentation, risk taking, and perseverance were singled out for reward. Our reward system thus sent a clear message that we assigned high value to active participation in the innovation process.

The use of rewards at King's College has also been effective in reinforcing faculty goodwill, professional pride, and dedication to educating students. I do not believe, however, that the use of rewards will result in sustained change if these more noble impulses are not already present among faculty members. The worst sort of environment for fostering successful innovation is one that reduces all faculty effort to the cash nexus. But it is equally true that those faculty members who consistently support and implement desired new measures need to know that their efforts are genuinely appreciated.

Conclusion

Not all change involves innovation. Some changes, for example, result from drift, or they may involve a shift to altered circumstances that are not in themselves new. Yet innovation (purposeful action taken to accomplish something new) frequently lies behind the most significant examples of change. Academic leaders who desire change or see its need must create environments that encourage innovative thinking and risk taking. Achieving successful change in higher education is not accidental. Effective new undertakings result from careful planning, supported by proven strategies for implementing and sustaining change. The successful change agent understands the difference between the implementation and the maintenance of new measures. Initiating change may upset the equilibrium of a college or a university, but sustaining a desirable innovation permits the achievement of a new equilibrium and a full realization of the intended benefits. Understanding the human dimensions of change contributes to success in both the implementation and the maintenance tasks. King's College serves as a useful example for those who wish to examine the dynamics of successfully planned change.

References

Seymore, D. T. Developing Academic Programs: The Climate for Innovation. Washington, D.C.: Association for the Study of Higher Education, 1988.
Tierney, W. G. "Organizational Culture in Higher Education: Defining the Essentials." Journal of Higher Education, 1988, 59 (1), 2-21.

D. W. Farmer is vice-president and dean of academic affairs at King's College, Pennsylvania, and was for ten years its chief planning officer.

Changing the corporate culture of a college or university is a
complex undertaking and a task that must often be accomplished
to enable innovations in mission, programs, organizational structure,
and ways of conducting institutional affairs.

Changing the Corporate Culture

James B. Kashner

The culture of contemporary American higher education and of the institutions comprising it consists of a unique blend of traditional values, norms, and folkways that define its character and influence the behavior of its members. Emerging with universities in medieval Europe, this culture has enjoyed a long history. It has maintained its essential characteristics, sustained its core values and traditions, and warded off intrusions from the outside for nearly a millennium. Itself the product of evolution, it has nevertheless nourished a sense of traditionalism that is often antithetical to change.

The traditional nature of the university community is displayed most vividly when academia attempts to adjust either to public policy positions calling for change or to the fiscal and other realities that attend our era of social, political, and demographic change and of competition in higher education. Rooted in centuries of tradition, practice, and even pomp, the reigning college and university culture has been remarkably resistant to the many social realities that currently press for change.

Exploding enrollments after 1945 prompted the creation of hundreds of new institutions of higher education, myriad new programs and curricula, and many structural changes in American colleges and universities. But the value system at the heart of academic culture remained fundamentally the same. Even now these values continue to be so important as to warrant the statement that academia—in terms of its essential mission, its traditional assumptions and ideals, its cherished habits of autonomy, its customary arrangements as to governance and faculty authority in the conduct of institutional affairs, and the historic centrality of the liberal arts disciplines in the curriculum—remains under the sway of a traditional culture that stubbornly opposes innovation. The question at present is whether or not new global and national circumstances will bring about basic change—or, more pointedly, whether or not the persons responsible for higher education will find ways to adapt its culture to these new circumstances.

The Culture of Higher Education

The culture of contemporary American higher education, like that of its antecedents, rests on governing assumptions about the important role of education and the way that academic institutions should be operated; on a special set of values, beliefs, and norms that constrain behavior in colleges and universities; on a well-defined cluster of roles and statuses that offer intrinsic rewards for academicians; and on a set of meaningful symbols through which actions and loyalties are focused. Together, these elements constitute the essence of academic culture. Separately, each is internalized by members of the academic community in ways that materially affect their behavior and often render it hostile to change. Readying an institution to reply to conditions that call for change or to innovate on the institution's own initiative requires a clear understanding of its corporate culture and of how to modify that culture in a desired direction.

Governing Assumptions and Special Values. Centuries of social tradition accord colleges and universities great regard as the chief vehicle for instruction in the historic liberal arts, as the primary provider of advanced learning in the realms of general and specialized knowledge, and as the principal educational means toward a better life for citizens. So regarded, higher education occupies a special place in our society's definitions of truth, value, and worth. The distinctive regard in which academia is held confers special status on it and reinforces the influence of the customary values with which it is associated. This is so even though new circumstances—such as a persistent demand from student customers for preparation to enter careers, which is antithetical to the old liberal education ideal that learning should be prized for its own sake—clash with what is traditional. The innovator in higher education must thus proceed from an understanding of the ways in which novel conditions interplay with the inherited academic culture and must seek to find a means of reconciling the two so as to enable change.

Among the assumptions concerning colleges and universities, one of the most important is that the enterprise of higher education should be unrestrained by forces external to it. This conception of the unfettered academy may reflect a worthy ideal, but the present reality is that academic managers must deal with social calls for accountability, with the demands of the consumers of higher education, and with budgetary constraints and the need to position their institutions strategically for the future. Innovators in higher education must find effective counters to the ideal of the unfettered—or, better, the isolated and self-contained—campus as one important means of modifying the corporate culture so as to empower change.

Roles and Statuses. All cultures possess a system of defined roles and statuses that, in turn, prescribe superordination and subordination as individuals interact. Every major organizational theorist has thus found it necessary to discuss the importance of role and status configurations in the shaping of organizations. One familiar theme in these discussions is that the presence of formally defined roles and statuses is a basic characteristic of bureaucratic organizations. It is also vital to note that individual members are bonded to their organization by the system of defined roles and statuses within it. The shared experiences of members of organizations, furthermore, place roles and statuses squarely in the realm of concrete value, as instruments that palpably structure the social worlds of, for example, colleges and universities.

Roles and statuses in the academic setting may also assume a sacrosanct symbolic place. For instance, the symbolic significance of faculty ranking has in large measure produced the informal social hierarchy of the contemporary campus, as well as its functional hierarchy. To the individual actor, advancement through the hierarchy of ranks holds real and substantial meaning, and the meaning is such that attainment of high rank or status becomes an intrinsic reward in and of itself.

Persons seeking to change institutions of higher education are well advised to make effective use of the all-important realities of roles and statuses. They can do this by providing for colleagues who support efforts to implement desired innovations, a system of rewards that is articulated with and reflects the hierarchy of desirable roles and statuses on a campus.

Symbolic Territories. The system of roles and statuses in the organization of higher education not only determines functions and relationships on campuses but also creates a set of symbols that amount to territories, spheres of ownership or privately held "turf" within colleges and universities. Supported by custom and habit and often by real practical considerations, various spheres of ownership may operate as potent points of resistance to change, especially if projected innovations appear to threaten the proprietors. Such territoriality extends beyond simple control of administrative units, pieces of buildings or campuses, or collections of individuals or functions. The practice of aggregating individuals who share interests—often forming subgroups within a single discipline—adds an element of social bonding to the mix, as do disciplinary rivalries and commonly held notions of disciplinary boundaries. Change agents must devise strategies for addressing this territorial component of the campus culture.

Traditionalism. Conceptually, it is useful to describe contemporary American institutions of higher education as traditional. The traditional character of academia is embedded deeply in colleges' and universities' views of themselves and in their social roles and the primary functions that society assigns to them. We have already noted some ways in which the historic values and elements of higher education are resistant to change. Perhaps La Piere (1965) was correct when he suggested that change in itself is undesirable and that the ideal social condition is stability. The prevalence of resistance to change lends behavioral authority to the view that the successful innovator must act as a sort of artist who can create a new order from disparate and often intractable raw materials.

Alignment of the Corporate Hierarchy

Every formal organization possesses a definitive hierarchical structure whose constituent elements perform specific functions and set up for themselves a normative framework for behavior. The hierarchies of colleges and universities typically contain at least four principal structural components: the governing board, the administration, the faculty, and the student body. Some institutions also accord formal hierarchical roles to professional or other staff groups. Like the institution itself, each constituent group consists of a hierarchy with its own conception of the campus and how it should function.

Governing Board. The governing board holds the ultimate responsibility for the welfare of the campus community. The boards of public institutions act under either constitutional or statutory authority as agents exercising a public trust. Those of private or independent institutions typically are the boards of directors of not-for-profit corporations chartered to operate institutions of higher education in the public interest. In both cases, boards perform broad policy-making functions that guide the institutions they govern. In both cases, boards hold the normative responsibility for setting the college's or university's direction and for maintaining its quality. In both, the art of board membership requires of governors the best of human qualities, among which dedication is one of the most important.

Boards of public institutions must act in conformity with public policy guidelines. In doing so, many presently are obliged to initiate or to encourage change in the institutions that they oversee. They act through the chief executive officer of the campus, whose initiatives are the means of giving effect to their decisions and directives. Just now, public governing boards are directing increasing attention toward strategic planning, while maintaining customary interest in the familiar spectrum of campus program activities, in tuition levels, and in capital improvements. Where tax revenues are dwindling or growing too slowly, the role of public governing boards is assuming greater significance than formerly. Governing bodies in such instances may turn to an increasingly intrusive style of direction, extending their authority beyond policy making toward management, as they seek to ensure what they believe to be a wise use of scarce institutional resources.

Like their public counterparts, the boards of private institutions are legally and morally responsible for broad policy determinations as well as for general oversight of campus affairs. They also consider proposals for new program initiatives and provide, as seems appropriate, assistance in positioning colleges or universities for the future. They add a further vital function: In their capacity as corporate directorates, they solicit and contribute both capital and operating funds. Insofar as governing bodies of private or independent institutions actively direct campus affairs, they act, like those in the public sector, through the chief executive officer.

Administration. The administrative team gives effect to the policy directives of the board and, charged with conducting the ongoing affairs of the institution, acts as the actual key change agent on campus. It is the administrative team, appointed by the governing board, that must work within and at times seek to transform the various elements of the campus culture. Administrators must be both initiators and managers of change.

The problem, of course, is to translate effort into the accomplishment of desired change. Success requires, first, that administrators be willing to lead. They must be willing to enter into dialogue with their colleagues, to articulate the institution's mission, to communicate convincingly the policy position of the campus, and, most of all, to make decisions, some of which may not be greeted with enthusiasm. To perform these functions effectively demands well-developed skills in communication, negotiation, and interpersonal relations, as well as sensitivity to cherished campus values. The essence of the craft of leadership is to employ these skills in ways that invite sympathetic, if not enthusiastic, campus perceptions of leaders and of their motives and actions.

Faculty. The faculty enjoys the legitimate campus role that carries the longest history and the greatest traditional respect in the culture of higher education. Because the faculty performs the focal role in academia, its reaction to any contemplated change is crucial. The wise change agent knows this and attempts, in devising a change strategy, to estimate with care the impact of projected innovations on the faculty and the likely faculty perception of that impact. As a general principle, the addition of new academic programs will be more acceptable than the redirection or reduction of programs, provided that the proposed additions do not demonstrably direct resources away from established programs or otherwise appear to menace them. The faculty is also likely to bear a primary responsibility for effecting educational changes and thus to perceive them as threatening. This is particularly the case where program redirection, program reduction, or a reallocation of resources is the issue. For these reasons, whatever the particulars of a given case, it is axiomatic that the cultivation of faculty support is ordinarily essential for successful program innovation and for change of other sorts in areas of faculty concern.

It is important to emphasize here that the faculty component of the campus hierarchy, with its normal inertia and human tendency to prefer the familiar, is not necessarily or automatically inclined to resist change, although this statement may surprise readers who are familiar with faculty intransigence in the face of innovation. Nor are faculties necessarily disposed to favor change, although here and there one may find campus cultures that value innovation and experimentation. What makes the most sense is to conceive of the faculty as a necessary component in any projected initiative. Faculty involvement in change is indispensable and must be assiduously cultivated. Without this involvement, contrived in such a fashion as to grant the faculty shared ownership, a campus is virtually assured that discussion of change will take place in a context of internal conflict. While conflict may in some instances be unavoidable, it is generally a good idea to pick battles carefully and to avoid skirmishes that can divert energy from the task of winning support for major proposals.

Students. The final component of the typical campus hierarchy is the student consumer. The student consumer is or ought to be the chief beneficiary of most educational change. Often she or he is also the party most likely to suffer adverse effects from projected program changes. And the modern student consumer is much more likely than his or her predecessors to discern a direct connection between academic or other program changes and the accomplishment of educational objectives that are, in turn, linked to important career goals. The contemporary student, moreover, is much more likely than earlier generations of students to express concerns about planned changes. All of these facts point clearly to the need for students to be drawn into the process of considering innovations.

Participatory Process. Each of these groups—governing boards, administrators, faculty, and students—is a stakeholder with a vested interest in the organization. It follows that change agents must devise strategies that work with, rather than against, this reality of college and university organization and culture. Here and there local custom may sanction a genuinely democratic approach to innovation, granting voice and vote to all constituent groups. In the main, though, what is called for is a broadly participatory, representative, and consultative process that provides information for and solicits opinion from groups across the campus while reserving the actual leadership and decision-making tasks for those ordinarily expected to act: the administration and the faculty. Recourse to an open process, with a proper regard for established ways of making decisions, can yield the consensus required for change while respecting the established governance arrangements. Even where extraordinary circumstances demand a departure from normal governance practice, it is advisable to employ a broadly participatory process in tandem with strong administrative leadership.

Reshaping the Culture to Enable Institutional Change

Completely changing a college or a university or effecting almost any change within a campus is a complex, demanding, and delicate task. As we have seen, change involves interactions with values and habits embedded in the academic culture at large as well as with the ways of a particular institution and with the constituent elements of a campus hierarchy. Often, approval for initiatives or for alterations in programs, institutional direction, campus policies, and the like cannot be won unless it is preceded by some enabling changes in the campus culture. In other words, desired innovations may be attainable only if the values and habits that influence behavior and reward activity are altered in such a way as to permit the innovations to be perceived favorably.

Planning. I do not believe that desirable organizational or institutional changes are natural, inevitable, or recurring. Rather, they are *possible*, and their accomplishment is the result of a rational process. Successful efforts to change depend on design, planning, and purposeful execution. It is planning that promises innovations that will best serve the needs of relevant campus constituencies. For planning to be most fruitful, there must be an assignment of the planning function to an individual or a group. Often the word *planning* elicits a chorus of groans or an epidemic of yawns when it is uttered in an academic community. Where this is the case, the first order of business will be to change the campus culture so as to make the notion of planning acceptable, if not important. Provision of workshops, presentations by expert consultants, funding for attendance at conferences, and stipends for special planning activities are all proven means of enlisting support for planning. Also useful may be efforts to co-opt one or more key campus leaders to serve on planning bodies. Financial or other incentives or rewards may work well here. A more comprehensive approach is to incorporate into the campus compensation and promotion programs a performance evaluation component that assesses and rewards planning activity.

Goal Setting. Another element of the local culture that may require alteration before desired institutional changes can be achieved may be an antipathy to setting goals. Where this attitude is present, the change agent will need to look hard again at the reward system in order to see whether or not modifications might encourage a favorable shift of views. One of the most potent tools for replacing a business-as-usual spirit is the linkage of rewards— such as increases in compensation, advancement in rank or status, recognition, or eligibility for support to pursue desired projects—with the achievement of goals set out in an annual individual performance plan. Recourse to the use of such plans, by the way, can often foster a spirit of cooperation between supervisors and subordinates or colleagues by placing the former in the role of allies in the attainment of goals. Goal setting itself is a vital attitudinal component of any successful attempt to implement change.

Inertia and a Sense of Powerlessness. If the experiences of an institution nourish a conviction that change is impossible or that the members of the campus community are powerless either to effect change or to make a difference, then it will be crucial to contrive experiences that foster confidence in the ability to innovate. Small successes can build confidence and allay a sense of powerlessness, in the process weakening inertia. The particular courses chosen to accomplish these small successes will vary with local circumstances.

Complacency. There are campuses where complacency, a smug self-satisfaction or sense of superiority, or deeply entrenched ways of doing things oppose all change as unwise, unnecessary, or even as a venture into unwarranted experimentalism. This element of campus culture may be effectively addressed through the provision of carefully researched information, which faculties in particular often find to be persuasive. Dispatch of investigative teams to other campuses, provision of funding to send key persons to workshops or conferences, establishment of support for on-campus forums and the like may all serve to improve the flow of information and to cultivate a climate that is intrinsically more receptive to innovation.

New Personnel. Finally, one must always remember that higher education is an intensely human enterprise. Individual human beings espouse and perpetuate the attitudes and practices comprising an institution's culture. To the extent that it is possible to inject into the system new personnel selected in part because they hold values consistent with the new directions contemplated for the institution, change managers can tip the balance more decisively toward innovation. It will be no less important, after recruiting the new personnel, to reward them for acting in desired ways and to employ them as allies in building a consensus around new or transformed values.

College of the Southwest

The experience of College of the Southwest (CSW) since 1987 illustrates how changing an institution's culture can enable other changes that revitalize it. A planning process was the centerpiece of our efforts. Through it we found ways to weaken traditional turf claims, nourish an institution-wide perspective, replace a sense of faculty powerlessness with a more optimistic spirit, and achieve a coherence of curriculum and policies that was previously lacking.

Founded as recently as 1962, CSW is one of only three private institutions of higher education in New Mexico. Besides the problems facing all of academia, CSW confronts several difficulties of its own. It serves a sparsely inhabited region. The local economy is subject to a boom-and-bust cycle characteristic of the two major local industries, petroleum and plains agriculture. The regional population is highly mobile and fluctuates with business conditions; it has been down sharply in recent years. The college is practically unendowed and thus is driven by tuition and enrollment. A tiny student body, less than 240 strong, renders the institution especially vulnerable. By 1987, a decline of nearly 20 percent in enrollment, inadequate classroom and laboratory equipment, thin staffing, and several

years of administrative drift had resulted in CSW's being placed on probation by the North Central Association of Colleges and Schools (NCA).

A new administration arrived in 1987, determined, with the full support of the governing board, to mend affairs. A long-range planning effort
began almost immediately, leading to the revitalization of the institution in
twenty-six months. Strong administrative leadership, a broadly participatory
process, and an ample flow of information worked together to advance
planning. Through sharing in the task of planning, faculty members learned
to abandon a discipline-based perspective and embrace an understanding
of the needs of the entire institution. Completion of the plan, in turn,
encouraged the faculty to replace pessimism and a deep-rooted sense of
powerlessness with a sense of possibility born of empowerment. The introduction and use of a merit pay system, a faculty development fund, public
praise, and other rewards to recognize the accomplishment of goals established in the plan helped nourish implementation and continuing progress.
An arts and sciences core took shape, providing a new level of curricular
coherence in the place of the former discipline-specific and largely inco-
herent set of degree requirements. The appointment of new faculty and
professional staff members sympathetic to the aims of the plan furthered
the transformation of CSW, now animated by a culture much more receptive to change than the former culture had been. Our efforts led the NCA to
lift probation in recognition of our progress. In brief, we used the planning
process as the chief means of transforming CSW's culture and then of
setting the college back on the road to health.

Conclusion

The corporate culture of higher education in general, as well as that of
individual campuses, is a crucial reality that those seeking to introduce
change must confront. Frequently, changes in the corporate culture must
occur *before* other changes—in mission, programs, ways of conducting
institutional affairs, college and university structure—can gain any prospect
of success. Administrators seeking to make changes may find several pieces
of advice helpful as they plan how to proceed.

1. Any campus change agent must begin with a thorough understanding of the local institutional culture. She or he must grasp the core values
and know which priorities are most revered as a necessary prelude to any
successful venture into innovation.

2. Change-minded administrators must discern clearly how projected
measures fit into or depart from the campus culture. This knowledge will
make it possible to determine where the culture itself may need to be
altered and which elements of the culture favor the desired undertaking.

3. It is always important to be informed about which campus constituencies, which elements of the role and status hierarchy, and which groups

of individuals most strongly support which elements of the campus culture. Such information is invaluable in considering what the politics—and the political maneuvering room—of a specified alteration of the campus culture might be. Innovators must be able to foresee potential areas of controversy and to identify primary centers of both support and resistance so as to be able to plan how best to work with the former and deal with the latter.

4. There is no substitute for clarity in planning and setting goals or for clear and effective communication of plans, goals, and the reasons for which these plans and goals are made.

5. Honesty and compassion in addressing issues are critically important for establishing and maintaining the credibility of initiators of change.

6. The manager who does not exercise foresight in preparing to deal with the positive and negative outcomes of projected innovations—that is, the manager who does not anticipate *all* of the major outcomes—courts failure.

7. Innovators must hold to their priorities firmly. To stake all on the outcome of a battle over a minor issue is to risk losing all.

8. Change agents must listen. Academic institutions exist to widen the realm of knowledge and to teach. We can all learn from the insights of colleagues and from experience. A participatory process can amplify opportunities for listening and for learning. It can also enlarge the possibilities for wise decision making.

University and college officers who heed these bits of advice position themselves to lead intelligently, sensitively, firmly, and collegially. These are the qualities of leadership on which successful efforts to innovate— and on which the very success of colleges and universities in a rapidly changing world—depend.

Reference

La Piere, R. T. *Social Change.* New York: McGraw-Hill, 1965.

James B. Kashner is vice-president for academic affairs at College of the Southwest, Hobbs, New Mexico.

Revision of a college's or university's mission statement through use of a broadly participatory process can provide a new and sharpened sense of direction and priorities and thus act as a powerful mechanism for institutional change.

Revising the Institutional Mission

Charles A. Dominick

The concept of institutional mission in higher education is variously defined and understood. Textbook discussions usually treat institutional mission as the sum of three components: teaching, research, and service. One or another of these (perhaps one or more) receives greater emphasis, depending on the size and type of institution. Large public universities usually embrace all three as equally important elements of their mission. Regional institutions tend to focus more on teaching and service and less on research. Some nationally visible universities, both public and private, characterize themselves as primarily research universities. Small liberal arts colleges usually emphasize their teaching function and frequently express their institutional mission in terms of student development; they describe the expected outcomes or goals in language that reflects a commitment to offering students an education of the "whole person"—that is, intellectual, spiritual, esthetic, moral, and physical instruction.

Those who are knowledgeable about higher education sometimes dismiss institutional mission statements as mere boilerplate material used to fill the opening pages of catalogues or the initial paragraphs of promotional brochures. The rhetoric of such statements too often seems to be high-sounding but essentially meaningless; in effect, it seems to be the academic equivalent of an affirmation of motherhood, apple pie, and the American way. To the extent that the mission statement of a given institution closely resembles those of other similar institutions, the statement may be thought of as unimaginative and of limited value. Yet it should not be surprising that similar institutions describe their missions in similar ways or that the great majority of all mission statements seem to be pretty much like one another. After all, colleges and universities do

NEW DIRECTIONS FOR HIGHER EDUCATION, no. 71, Fall 1990 ©Jossey-Bass Inc., Publishers

share many goals in common, whatever the differences in their particular circumstances and heritages.

To be truly useful, however, a statement of mission must somehow move beyond describing generic functions or merely listing institutional goals that are indistinguishable from the goals of other institutions. Mission is purpose. A statement of mission is a statement of intent, of direction. It serves as a guide for institutional decision making. A college or university that is clear about its mission can more easily choose among competing goals and can more readily establish its priorities than can one that is uncertain about its mission. Institutional consensus about mission can provide focus, meaning, and vision. It is this last that is most important. What finally distinguishes one campus from another is the extent to which a college or a university allows its sense of mission, which embodies its vision of and for itself, to influence its planning and to guide its actions. A well-articulated and successfully embodied statement of purpose can essentially define an institution.

Confusion about institutional mission exists when the various constituencies of a campus hold disparate views about basic goals. If trustees, faculty members, students, administrators, alumni, and other constituents disagree about a college or a university's direction, there is likely to be little consensus to support major decisions affecting programs or organizational changes. A problem that many campuses must at some point in their history confront is that a number of separate groups with legitimate interests project incompatible, or at least different, futures for their institutions. Bringing together these diverse views of institutional mission and reconciling them as much as possible require major efforts at consensus building.

A Case Study: Wittenberg University

Wittenberg University in Springfield, Ohio, is an example of an institution that has successfully restated its mission so as to reflect more closely a new consensus on institutional direction and purpose. When William Kinnison was chosen as the eleventh president of Wittenberg in 1975, he was aware that the university did not possess sufficient resources to meet every expectation and to fund every dream of its various constituencies. Kinnison observed in his inaugural address that the university must move beyond defining its aspirations as the sum or composite of everyone's wants and away from the premise that something for everyone was an adequate institutional vision or operating principle.

Founding Aims. In its 130 years of operation, Wittenberg had embraced several different visions. The university originated in 1845 as Wittenberg College. Its founders conceived the college's primary mission to be the Americanization of a German Lutheran immigrant community. This mission was to be accomplished by training an English-speaking clergy for the German Lutheran parishes of the region and by meeting the broader educational needs of the German immigrants. Unlike many nineteenth-century colleges founded by clergy, Wittenberg never existed solely to provide theological training. In fact, from the beginning the college emphasized both the traditional classical curriculum and the study of science and modern languages, as well as theology. Business and political economy were incorporated into the curriculum in the 1860s, and art, music, physical education, and teacher training were added in the 1870s. The theological department of the college was organized as a seminary in 1889.

University Status. Wittenberg College became Wittenberg University in 1959, following a two-year study conducted by the faculty and the board of directors. The study concluded that there was a need in higher education for a type of institution somewhere between the small, liberal arts colleges and the much larger, comprehensive universities. Wittenberg University emerged with an organizational structure that included the College of Arts and Sciences; the School of Professional Studies, which contained programs in business administration, education, home economics, medical technology, nursing, art, music, and religious studies; the School of Community Education, to serve adult learners in the local community; the Hamma Divinity School; and the Graduate Studies Program, which granted a master of education degree. There was serious discussion about eventually adding schools of law and medicine. The new university envisioned growing from a small college enrollment of 1,800 to a small university enrollment of around 5,000.

Challenges in the Sixties. With a change in administration in the 1960s, Wittenberg University again underwent reorganization. The College of Arts and Sciences and the School of Professional Studies merged to form Wittenberg College. The newly constituted college emphasized the liberal arts. Home economics, nursing, and medical technology were dropped from the curriculum. The School of Community Education continued in existence under the leadership of a jurisdictional dean. The Graduate Studies Program was phased out. A professional degree-granting School of Music, with its own dean, came into being. The Hamma Divinity School became the virtually autonomous Hamma School of Theology, with a separate president and board of directors. The university revised its estimate of an optimal total enrollment to around 2,800.

Competing Visions and a Clarification of Mission. As Wittenberg entered the 1970s, differing views as to mission, institutional character, and long-term goals still existed. Some of the university's constituencies still envisioned the emergence of a small comprehensive university with undergraduate and professional programs, while others insisted that Wittenberg should commit its resources to becoming a high-quality liberal arts college for undergraduates only. It was clear to Wittenberg's new president in the fall of 1975 that the issue could be resolved only through a careful and thorough process of achieving consensus. Kinnison sought the approval of such a process from the institution's board of directors. He recommended the appointment of a fourteen-member commission to study and define the school's mission and priorities. The board endorsed the project. Subsequently, the idea won approval at a university-wide president's retreat of faculty members, student representatives, and administrators.

Commission on Mission and Priorities. The Commission on Mission and Priorities (CMP), when fully constituted, consisted of fourteen members, six advisory members, and four ex-officio members. Of the fourteen regular members, one was the president, four were faculty representatives elected by the faculty, four were students selected by the student government association, three were members of the governing board selected by the chair of the board of directors, and two were administrative staff members appointed by the president. The governing board members appointed to the commission were deliberately selected to provide representation for the Lutheran church constituency, the alumni, and the local community. One of the board members was also the parent of a Wittenberg student.

The president designated vice-presidential-level administrators as advisory members of the CMP and asked them to serve both as resources and as active participants in the various task forces that the commission created. The ex-officio members included the chair of the board of directors, the presidents of the two Lutheran church synods that supported Wittenberg financially, and a representative of the national office of the Lutheran Church in America.

Presidential Leadership. As an indication of his total commitment to the project, Kinnison himself assumed the chair of the commission. He appointed an administrative staff member as project director to provide staff support, to record the CMP's deliberations, to manage its budget, to keep the commission within its timetable and charge, and to coordinate the efforts of the CMP and of the seven task forces that it formed. The Aid Association for Lutherans and the Lutheran Church in America furnished grants to help underwrite the expenses of the commission. The university also contributed matching funds.

Focused Efforts. The commission received a carefully prepared charge and a detailed timetable to guide its deliberations. It enjoyed complete freedom, however, to organize itself as it thought best for the performance of the duties assigned to it. It decided not only to address the issue of institutional mission but also to complete a thorough self-study of the university to support its consideration of mission. Fortunately, the CMP's activity coincided with the decennial reaccreditation review of the North Central Association of Colleges and Schools and ultimately served both to fulfill its charge and to prepare for the review. After surveying a mound of available reports, documents, and descriptive data, the CMP divided itself into seven functional task forces. These focused respectively on the educational mission of the university, campus life, the religious environment, enrollment trends, campus facilities, finances and resources, and university administrative structure and governance.

Preliminary Draft Statement. The commission's first task was to draft a preliminary statement of institutional mission that it would revisit at the end of its eighteen-month effort. Members wrote the draft statement at a two-day retreat, where they used a brainstorming technique to identify more than forty assumptions about the internal and external environments that they believed should inform the university's stated mission. They also authorized the use of the Educational Testing Service's Institutional Goals Inventory (IGI) to survey faculty, alumni, parent, and student perceptions about Wittenberg.

The CMP framed a preliminary set of goal statements against which to compare and interpret the results of the IGI. The group employed a modified Delphi technique for reviewing written reactions to proposed institutional goal statements as an aid in shaping the preliminary statement of mission. At the annual president's fall retreat that opened the 1976–77 academic year more than 100 faculty members, student representatives, and trustees subjected the draft statement and the list of assumptions on which it was based to open review, criticism, and discussion.

Task Force Activity. The longest phase of the CMP's activity was a six-month period during which the seven task forces were functioning. A different member of the commission chaired each task force. The groups contained, besides members of the CMP, an additional forty-five persons appointed to represent the faculty, the administration, the students, and various other of the university's constituencies. The charge to each task force was to assemble, examine, evaluate, and discuss available relevant data, to conduct appropriate research, and, after considering various options, to report findings and recommendations to the commission.

The task forces invested more than 300 hours in analyzing and discussing their respective areas of concern. No two groups worked exactly alike. Task forces employed on-campus interviews of groups and of individuals, surveys, reviews of current literature, use of outside consultants, and reviews of existing internal documents and data, including departmental self-studies and specially prepared position papers, as they prepared for the discussions that preceded completion of their reports. Nearly 150 individual students, faculty members, administrators, board members, parents, and alumni participated in interviews with task force members as work progressed. In addition, approximately 200 other individuals, on and off campus, responded to task force questionnaires and engaged in telephone interviews.

When the commission reconvened after six months of work by the task forces, it had in hand for its deliberations the preliminary statement of mission, the reports and recommendations of the task forces, the results of the Institutional Goals Inventory, and the findings of a national survey on images and expectations of colleges related to the Lutheran Church in America. Every Wednesday afternoon and evening for nearly six weeks the CMP met. During these sessions it heard reports, discussed findings, and drew together the basic components of its final report.

Brief, Cogent Report. One of the major concerns of the CMP throughout its deliberations was to produce a final report that the campus community would in fact read. Commission members fully appreciated the importance of the process by which Wittenberg was attempting to revise its mission and restate its priorities. They were also aware of the substantial curiosity and interest with which both critics and supporters on campus awaited the final results of the lengthy project. And they recognized, even so, that a too-long and too-ponderous document would receive less attention than was needed. From the beginning, the CMP insisted that it should not write a weighty document that would simply gather dust on the bookshelves of faculty members and administrators. Rather, the final report was to be brief, cogent, and designed visually to permit easy reading.

Mission Grounded in Student Development. The final report of the commission redefined the institutional mission in terms of student development. Reaffirming that Wittenberg should remain an independent, undergraduate, residential, church-related liberal arts institution, the CMP prefaced its mission statement with the assertion that "Wittenberg University's fundamental purpose is to help educate 'the creative minority of a civilization,' to develop in harmony the intellectual, spiritual, social, esthetic, and physical qualities which characterize wholeness of person" (Wittenberg University Commission on Mission and Priorities, 1977, p. 1).

Meaning of Uniqueness. Despite the months of deliberation, Wittenberg's statement of mission was not new or revolutionary. When a university strives mightily to rethink its reasons for being, it is likely to discover that it cannot write a statement that is totally new or that contains many previously unexpressed ideas. The uniqueness of an institution of higher education is subtle, difficult to discover, and once found and expressed is still easily missed in a cursory reading of a statement of mission.

Wittenberg's commission could not deny the tradition and ethos of the university. Neither could it always choose clearly one option over another when focusing on such issues as education primarily for the sake of intellectual development versus education to nourish wholeness of person, liberal education versus education as preparation for a career, instruction grounded in Judeo-Christian values as opposed to instruction to accomplish secular aims, teaching to encourage freedom and individuality in defining a mode of life as against teaching that stresses the restraints inherent in membership in social communities, and education that stresses democratic governance versus education that emphasizes responsibility for the well-being of institutions. In virtually all cases, the matter was one of balancing the various contending options in a way that was appropriate for Wittenberg as a particular institution. The issue was not so much to discover new or distinctive elements as it was to frame a suitable and distinctive balance.

New Balance. The uniqueness that was discovered for Wittenberg University's mission was evident not so much in the originality of the ideas presented in the statement of mission as it was in the balance struck among them. The individual elements of the mission were much less important than the synergistic relationships among and between them when they were set out as components of a larger whole. As important as the written statement was, the ways in which it would be embraced and embodied in all of the institution's decisions and actions were even more crucial. The report of the commission was a challenge to the university community. The commission in transmitting it amplified this quality by challenging all who were in positions of leadership among faculty, among students, among members of the governing board, and within the administration to read, to understand, and to interpret it to others and to cooperate with the president in its implementation.

Adoption and Results. The faculty and the governing board both formally adopted the new statement of purpose, the associated list of institutional priorities, and the related recommendations of the CMP. The commission fulfilled its promise, providing the Wittenberg community with a clear road map into the future. The people associated with Wittenberg have in turn given life to the statement and to the recommendations of the commission, employing them as bases for institutional decisions. The open process by which the CMP reached consensus, as it turned out, served also to build consensus among and within the university's various constituencies. While new issues still emerge and conflicting viewpoints continue to find expression, the campus community understands more clearly than before what it is, why it exists, and where it is going.

Wittenberg's efforts to revise institutional mission became at the same time a long-range planning activity that has served the campus well for more than a decade. Wittenberg has since used the commission process on two other occasions, employing first a commission on the status of the faculty and then a commission on the academic climate. Each new commission has built on the efforts of its predecessors, incorporating into its work the understandings and recommendations of earlier commissions where appropriate. The consensus forged by means of the commission process guides the deliberations of key faculty boards and committees as well as the annual strategic planning activities of the president's administrative team.

Essential Elements

Wittenberg University's experience suggests that a revision of institutional mission can be accomplished successfully when a number of conditions are met. The following are among the most important:

1. There is strong leadership within the administration, committed to the task of building a consensus for change.
2. The administration actively supports revision and provides budgetary resources sufficient to underwrite the costs associated with it.
3. The institution's governing board endorses and is committed to the revision process.
4. The revision effort involves representatives of all major campus constituencies, especially the faculty, the students, and the alumni.
5. The activity allows for open communication and dialogue between and within all relevant constituencies.
6. Use is made of extant reports, data, and information-gathering and storage systems to provide a sound basis for recommendations.
7. The process provides adequate time for group-building activities and the development of commitment to the outcomes.
8. There is an understanding of the steps for implementation, and there is provision for periodic evaluation of the results.
9. There is a natural occasion for change, such as the beginning of a new presidency.

Revision of mission may occur under many different circumstances. For some campuses, it may take place in response to a need to refocus or sharpen a long-held sense of purpose. For others, it may reply to external or internal conditions that threaten institutional survival or that hold out unusual opportunities. For still others, it may result from a desire on the part of the president, the governing board, or the faculty to redirect a college or university's energies and resources. The local circumstances may influence the process of revision as well as the shape of the final statement of purpose. The method of revision described in this chapter worked well in a situation that was essentially stable and in which disagreements about future directions had not rendered the institution immobile.

Wittenberg University's Commission on Mission and Priorities came to view itself as a prototype, a model for achieving consensus about purpose, for other institutions to emulate. To embrace the same approach, an institution must accept, as Wittenberg did, the premises that consensus on mission is necessary, that it is desirable, and that it is possible.

Reference

Wittenberg University Commission on Mission and Priorities. *Report of the Wittenberg University Commission on Mission and Priorities.* Springfield, Ohio: Wittenberg University, 1977.

Charles A. Dominick is vice-president for institutional relations at Wittenberg University.

The redirection of resources is an effective means of replying to institutional decline and of managing conditions for growth.

Allocating Resources as a Means of Inducing and Responding to Change

Keith W. Mathews

The real resources employed in institutions of higher education include people, land and buildings, books and other information media, equipment, and materials and supplies. The principal unit of measure, of course, is money, although position authorization lists are also common. Significant educational change in a college or university frequently involves at least some redirection of resources. The change may or may not cause, or even result from, an increase or decrease in the total amount of resources available.

Managing Higher Education's Resources

The administrations and boards of colleges and universities do not fully control the resources available to them. Political and public relations considerations require attention. Even more limiting may be legally enforceable requirements imposed by private donors or government funding entities. Institutional accounting systems provide records of these legal requirements through the technique of fund accounting. Fund accounting classifies resources into groups according to the restrictions placed on them. The fund groups generally used by colleges and universities are current, loan, endowment and similar, annuity and life income, plant, and agency funds.

Unrestricted funds provide the maximum flexibility. These may be used for any purpose. They are the basis for the annual operating budget. Usually, current operations consume most of them. However, institutions may move unrestricted funds from the current fund group to other groups as long as unrestricted funds remain designated as such within those other groups.

Donors of restricted funds may specify current or capital purposes. Restricted current funds supplement unrestricted funds in the annual operating budget, but they may be used only as the donors specify. Restricted capital funds may feed the endowment or physical plant fund group. The donors of endowment funds require the institutions to invest the principal amount and use only the investment income currently. The investment income may be restricted or unrestricted as to purpose. When institutions voluntarily add current funds to their endowment investments, these funds become "quasi-endowments" or "funds functioning as endowment," either restricted or unrestricted. Donors give plant funds for the acquisition of grounds, buildings, or equipment. Often, the donors specify the building or type of equipment that they wish to help finance.

Other types of restricted funds may benefit various constituents of a college or university. Loan funds become part of the student financial aid package. Annuity and life income funds provide a financial return to their donors until the donors' death or voluntary release. Commonly resulting from fund-raising solicitations, they are sometimes called "deferred gifts." Finally, institutions may administer agency funds on behalf of student, alumni, or other related groups or organizations.

When making spending decisions, especially in connection with the annual operating budget, higher education managers consider the functions to be performed, the organizational units that perform them, and the objects of expenditure. Commonly used current fund functions are instruction, research, public service, academic support, student services, institutional support, plant operation and maintenance, student financial aid grants, mandatory transfers (usually for debt retirement or grant matching), and auxiliary enterprises (such as residence and dining halls, campus bookstore, and so on). Organizational units are colleges, schools, and departments. Objects of expenditure include salaries, wages, books, equipment, and so on.

Unrestricted funds result primarily from tuition, fees, and state appropriations, but also from gifts, endowment earnings, and miscellaneous sources. All are initially recorded as current fund revenues. Unrestricted funds can freely cross functional and organizational lines so that the business administration division can subsidize the music conservatory (and usually does), while the bookstore margin can go toward faculty salaries. Nonmandatory transfers can carry unrestricted funds not needed for current operations to any of the other fund groups. Both the increase in the unrestricted current fund balance and the amount of nonmandatory transfers out of unrestricted current funds into quasi-endowment and plant funds during an operating period measure an institution's financial strength and flexibility.

Restricted funds can occasionally present management dilemmas, but even here institutions often have more control than is apparent on the surface. It is unusual for a donor to make the restrictions so tight that the institution either cannot use the funds at all or cannot do so without altering some objective. Often a donor will specify only an organizational unit, a function, or an object of expenditure without further limits or details. Thus, a gift restricted for research, for the music conservatory, or for faculty salaries presents little or no management difficulty. A gift for financial aid grants to conservatory students majoring in oboe recruited from a specified high school and with a 3.5 grade point average might sit unclaimed for a while. In such a case, the institution would try to persuade the donor to broaden the terms of this gift.

In fact, institutional fund raisers strongly influence donor restrictions. Gifts do not simply come in; institutions ask for them. They seek restricted gifts to pay for institutional needs—a specific building, department, or financial aid endowment, for example. Professional fund raisers approach donors with a variety of institutional needs, hoping that one of the needs will be of interest and will produce a gift.

This chapter examines resource decisions made within this framework of funds, restrictions, and needs—resource decisions that have influenced change within institutions of higher education. Two comprehensive examples will be provided, one of an institution that altered its management of resources in order to reverse successfully a serious decline in enrollment, the other of an institution that sought to control and manage conditions brought about by enrollment growth. The conclusion looks at the role of revenue in resource decisions.

Managing Resources to Reverse Institutional Decline

In the fall of 1982, Ohio Wesleyan University experienced a sharp decline in the number of entering new students. By fall 1985, enrollment at this central Ohio liberal arts institution had fallen from 2,200 to 1,300. From that low, it had returned to 1,800 by fall 1989. Maintenance for over a decade before 1982 of a relatively stable enrollment of 2,200 to 2,400 mostly full-time and residential students, together with reasonably conservative financial management, had provided some financial reserves. The reserves helped the university weather the enrollment crisis and allowed it to undertake innovative programs that aided the recovery.

Cutting Costs. The university's first response to the drop in enrollment came in the summer of 1982 with a plan for significant reductions in expenditures of unrestricted current funds. Campus leaders decided early, however, to avoid drastic cuts that would weaken operations or morale. They reasoned that such results would compound the enrollment difficulties.

Personnel Retrenchments. Because Ohio Wesleyan, like higher education in general, is labor intensive, cost cutting hit staffing levels in both faculty and administration. The faculty cuts involved the phasing out of seventeen out of 155 full-time positions and the elimination of another seven full-time equivalents, representing about half of the part-time positions. Many of these were individual posts in large departments held by untenured faculty members. The university also eliminated two small departments, community studies and speech, with the tenured positions that they contained. Mergers combined several other small departments into two larger ones: physics and astronomy, and modern foreign languages. Additional curricular changes occurred in journalism, education, and physical education. Comparable reductions occurred in most nonacademic areas. The business affairs vice president assumed the treasurer's functions. Computing held steady, while the admissions budget predictably increased. One residence hall closed. The university later converted the building into senior citizen rental housing.

Faculty Involvement in Retrenchment Decisions. Since the 1950s, Ohio Wesleyan had developed a culture of strong faculty involvement in campus governance. An elaborate elected committee structure existed, and regularly scheduled monthly faculty meetings often lasted three or four hours. Even minor issues often prompted extensive debate. This faculty influence ensured that drastic cuts would be avoided throughout the crisis and that any steps taken would receive thorough consideration from a broad spectrum of faculty members and administrators. Formal faculty approval of academic cuts in an August special meeting came only after an elected ad hoc faculty committee had taken positions on recommendations framed by a presidential ad hoc committee appointed earlier.

The elected committee used eleven publicly stated criteria in deciding on academic program reductions. The committee did not assign an order or a weight to the items on the list. The eleven criteria included the following:

- Basic ingredient of traditional liberal arts education: Is the discipline an important part of liberal arts exposure?
- Importance to the ambience of a quality liberal arts college: Does the discipline provide a noncurricular ambience to the college?
- Relation to high-priority programs in the college: Does this department serve or support college programs or other disciplines that are high-priority disciplines?
- Quality of students attracted to the program: Do students in the program, as a group, perform at an average or higher level?
- Student interest—voluntary, required: Is the discipline heavily enrolled? If so, is it by choice or by requirement? How many students elect this discipline as a major?
- Specific drawing power: Do students come to Ohio Wesleyan because this particular program is offered?

- Quality of program: Do students and faculty generally perceive the program to be of high quality?
- Quality of faculty in the program: Are faculty in the program, as a group, of high quality?
- Grade distribution in the department: Does the department grade differently in a significant way from the pattern of the college as a whole?
- Career orientation—current and future: Do students who major or minor in the discipline have special career opportunities?
- Cost: How does this department or program compare with others in terms of total cost, cost per graduation unit generated, and cost per student served?

This approach was similar to retrenchment steps taken recently at other institutions. For example, Hyatt, Shulman, and Santiago (1984) found large state-supported universities using one or more committees to target areas for cuts after conducting an institution-wide program review. In some cases they reallocated part of the resources saved to other programs considered to be vital to the institution's strength.

Budget-cutting efforts continued at Ohio Wesleyan for the next four years. These imposed further position reductions, held pay raises for continuing employees below the inflation rate, and tightly limited departmental budgets for costs other than payroll. However, these measures did not offset the significant reductions in tuition revenue, leaving Ohio Wesleyan to balance its annual budgets by other means.

Using Accumulated Resources to Balance the Budget. Conservative management practices over the years had provided the university with significant financial resources on which it could draw to balance the current operating budget during the period of difficulty.

Cumulative Operating Surplus. Many years of modest operating surpluses had given the university an accumulated balance of unrestricted current funds of $650,000 as of June 30, 1982. This reserve was the first to go.

Unrestricted Bequests. Under generally accepted accounting principles for colleges and universities, unrestricted bequests are revenue of the current fund. Ohio Wesleyan had long followed a conservative policy of allocating all such bequests, regardless of size, equally between plant and quasi-endowment, employing nonmandatory transfers to build up its capital. It suspended the transfers beginning with the 1982–83 fiscal year. Over the next three fiscal years, unrestricted bequests exceeding $1 million were used for current operations.

Endowment Management. Another conservative practice had been the use of the total-return concept for endowment management. Under a traditional approach stemming from trust law, many nonprofit organizations treat so-called ordinary income (dividends, interest, rents, and royalties) as spendable current income and treat all investment gains, both realized and unrealized, as increases of capital. This approach can cause instability in the annual budget, as dividend and interest rates fluctuate, or it can lead to investment management policies designed to produce stable ordinary income rather than maximum total return. Laws now adopted in many states permit educational institutions to use, instead, the total-return concept. This management approach frees investment policy from constraints involving ordinary income by allowing an institution to apply a formula to both ordinary income and a multiyear average of investment gains. Use of a multiyear average reduces the impact of market price fluctuations. The formula specifies a portion of ordinary income and investment gains to be spent currently. The institution reinvests the remainder to protect the purchasing power of the endowment principal from inflation.

In the early 1980s, the market experienced high interest rates. Use of the total-return approach enabled Ohio Wesleyan to transfer some ordinary income from current funds to endowment funds for reinvestment. After the enrollment decline, the university suspended these transfers and began spending all ordinary income currently. This change added about $250,000 to its current revenues in each of the next few years.

Withdrawal of Quasi-Endowment Funds. Finally, the university completed its budget balancing by making withdrawals from quasi-endowment funds through nonmandatory transfers to unrestricted current funds. Ohio Wesleyan's quasi-endowment funds had exceeded $5 million by June 30, 1982, the result primarily of its policy concerning unrestricted bequests and secondarily of a successful fund drive that ended on December 31, 1982. The campaign had garnered $33 million over ten years, $12 million for endowment and quasi-endowment, $11 million for plant, and $10 million for current use. It was ironic that the same financial report that heralded the drive's successful completion also announced the start of the enrollment decline.

Using Innovative Approaches. Along with these financial measures came new allocations of resources for innovative activities and a new emphasis on admissions, fund raising, public relations, and the academic program. Most interesting, from a resource management point of view, were an extensive merit scholarship venture and a specially financed, high-visibility speakers series.

Merit Scholarships. A prominent trustee first suggested an ambitious expansion of no-need merit scholarships. The university had in recent years been giving a small number of such awards, in addition to need-based financial aid that met a student's full need with a package of grant, loan, and part-time campus job. Now the university added fifty full- and half-tuition no-need awards for new students each year, starting in the fall of 1986. In the fall of 1989, a cumulative total of 182 awards was in effect. These awards have recruited honors students who otherwise would probably not have enrolled. Awards go to students in the top 10 percent of their secondary school classes who have combined Scholastic Aptitude Test (SAT) scores over 1100 or a composite American College Testing (ACT) score of at least 27. These standards are such that the awards probably do not displace tuition that would have otherwise been paid.

One argument for offering more merit scholarships was that they would cost little in the early years. This view rested on a type of cost-volume analysis common in financial management. Within a certain range of volume of activity (enrollment, in a university), costs have variable and fixed components. Variable costs fluctuate more or less proportionately with the level of activity; fixed costs do not. Fixed costs can change for many reasons but not because volume changes.

Because of the decision not to make drastic budget cuts, Ohio Wesleyan was deliberately operating with idle capacity, both in staff and in physical space. Existing class offerings could absorb another 50, 100, maybe 150 students. This condition made most educational and general costs fixed within an enrollment range of plus or minus 150 students. Variable educational and general costs would include only such minor items as stationery, duplicating, laboratory materials, and the like.

Variable costs are more significant in the auxiliary enterprise areas of colleges and universities. Here, they include food served in the dining halls and all products sold in the bookstore. Because the merit awards do not exceed tuition, recipients pay for auxiliary enterprise services. Their payments contribute to fixed costs and cover the added variable costs.

Ohio Wesleyan officials believe that this program has played a significant role in improving the academic climate and image of the university, raised average test scores, and helped attract other qualified students. They also know that as enrollment climbs into a new range, closer to capacity, more educational and general costs become variable. Thus, the awards will become an increasing burden in the budget.

National Colloquium. In 1984, a new president initiated the speakers series, a program for academic credit that he named the National Colloquium. It brings prominent (and high-priced) speakers to the campus to discuss issues of great national importance. Annual themes have included nuclear energy and weapons, population and the environment, the Constitution of the United States, and sports ethics. The program has stimulated significant campus intellectual activity and has been a good admissions and public relations device. Here, though, the added costs were immediately large: $144,000 the first year.

The budget could not absorb the full amount, but the colloquium attracted donor support. By allocating some unrestricted money to the series, the university was able to draw additional financing in the form of restricted current funds. Such mixing of restricted and unrestricted funds for a special project is a fairly common practice. When done at the institution's initiative, the unrestricted part is sometimes called "seed money." At times, donors take the initiative, making so-called matching or challenge grants that cover part, but not all, of an objective. The institution's matching money usually can come from either unrestricted funds or from other gifts restricted for the project.

Managing Resources to Sustain Institutional Growth

With full-time equivalent (FTE) enrollment reaching a new high each year in the mid 1980s, Baldwin-Wallace College (B-W) sought ways to absorb and sustain the growth without losing what had become a widely quoted institutional recruiting and public relations slogan: "A quality education with a personal touch." This comprehensive urban college in a southwest Cleveland suburb adds to the liberal arts a popular business administration division and a conservatory of music. The FTE enrollment of over 3,000 consists of 2,400 full-time and 2,000 part-time students, mostly from northern Ohio. Most of the part-time students pursue evening and weekend programs. There are two graduate degrees, the master of business administration and the master of education. Growth prompted leaders at B-W to raise questions, in the light of possible future enrollment size, that a large segment of higher education was also facing—questions about flexibility, salary levels, minority recruiting and enrollment, and the condition of certain campus facilities.

Flexibility. Although enrollment by the fall of 1988 had grown 30 percent over five years, the college remained concerned about the demographic projections for northern Ohio. With governing board backing, the administration continued the use of steps designed to provide future operating and financial flexibility. They cautiously, only where the need was compelling, added new full-time faculty or staff positions. They aggressively used part-time faculty, particularly in the evening and weekend programs, drawing on highly qualified persons from the Cleveland business community, a nearby National Aeronautics and Space Administration facility, and the Cleveland Orchestra for special expertise. They employed a formula requiring at least one nontenure-track full-time faculty appointment in most departments.

Even with strict hiring restraints, however, the average class size of around twenty-two was not unusually high for a private college.

Budgetary restraint had led to significant excesses of unrestricted current fund revenues over expenditures for many years. After building a $1 million balance in unrestricted current funds, the college began making nonmandatory transfers to plant funds in order to supplement plant fund gifts. Even after payments for significant plant renovations, unused transfers still provide a reserve for additional renovations or, in the worst case, budgetary problems. Since these funds remain unrestricted, a nonmandatory transfer back to current funds remains possible. Also available for transfer and use was a $4 million quasi-endowment balance.

Salaries. Given such financial strength, administrators, trustees, and faculty alike began to consider the level of college salaries. They all saw the higher enrollment as a result of faculty and staff efforts and recognized a need for still further effort to handle that enrollment. B-W's faculty salaries had for several years been rated 3 for all ranks in the annual salary survey of the American Association of University Professors (AAUP). Since employee benefits were more generous, total compensation won a 2 rating. Seeing a need to reward further the work being done, the administration and trustees, in consultation with the appropriate faculty committee, set a goal of increasing all salaries and wages so that faculty salaries would receive 2 ratings. They hoped to achieve this goal within two or three years after the 1987-88 fiscal year.

The rate of average increases in faculty salaries nationally compounded B-W's task in achieving its goal. The college's budgets in recent years had included pay raises, as well as tuition increases, at rates higher than the rate of inflation. In this, however, they were merely following much of higher education, as institutions generally tried to restore institutional and employee purchasing power lost in the 1970s. These trends continued through the 1988-89 academic year, despite a high level of public attention to the tuition increases. To move up one level in the AAUP ratings, the college would have to exceed average faculty raises given, probably for several years.

With the goal established, the administration developed as an analytical tool a preliminary budget model that highlighted the salary and wage increase percentage as a bottom-line item to be maximized. Now they prepare and discuss numerous versions of the model as they work on budget request guidelines for the coming year. Prepared on a personal computer, the model includes current-year data on enrollment, student fees, student financial aid component ratios, and condensed budgets for unrestricted current fund revenues, salaries and wages, and nonsalary and wages expenditures. It uses trial increase factors to calculate the same data elements for the coming year.

Using this device, the college set significant base pay increases for full-time faculty for 1988-89 and again for 1989-90. Accompanying these increases were tuition, room, and board hikes that were about average for private colleges in Ohio for those years. Allocations for noncompensation budget items were adequate to satisfy all reasonable departmental requests, and the college continued to meet the full need of financial aid students.

Minorities. Officials at Baldwin-Wallace have shared the growing national concern about the declining enrollments and high dropout rates of minority students and the limited number of minority persons in faculty and administrative positions. All of these conditions were evident at B-W, despite the presence of a long-continuing Upward Bound program, curricula dealing with issues of racism and sexism, and support of a black student cultural center.

A presidentially appointed task force concluded that the college must do more in the areas of faculty, staff, and student multicultural awareness. It should also improve support systems, orientation, peer mentoring, and financial assistance for minority students. To help bring these things about, the task force recommended creation of a position found in many higher education institutions, that of minority affairs director. The administration accepted this recommendation and has since filled the position.

In making this recommendation, the task force knew that establishing the new office was only a step toward real solutions, not a solution in itself. A significant number of colleges and universities already had such officials, and the task force had found widely varying opinions as to their accomplishments. Certain views, though, were widely held. Minority affairs officials needed the firm and consistent backing of top campus officers, adequate funding with which to work, and sufficiently high rank within the administration to achieve results. In agreeing to create the position, B-W's officers also committed themselves to this level of support.

The decision, then, carried with it an ongoing financial commitment, a commitment that must eventually be worked into the annual budget. As often happens with new programs in higher education, however, and even though this concept was not a new one, the college obtained significant grant support for the first two years. So, like the National Colloquium at Ohio Wesleyan, the minority affairs office at Baldwin-Wallace will initially operate on a mixture of restricted and unrestricted funds.

Facilities. During the 1980s, Baldwin-Wallace addressed facilities needs with a complex financial strategy. The strategy included a three-year fund-raising campaign, two separate tax-exempt first-mortgage bond issues, and the careful use of some of the nonmandatory transfers of unrestricted current funds already described.

The campaign began with a typical case statement, designed to attract and direct restricted gifts to college needs. The three-year goal, $15 million, was ambitious in light of B-W's fund-raising history and constituency. Of the goal, two-thirds was specified toward plant for two major projects plus other renovations and replacements. The balance was for endowment and current support. The amount actually raised was over $19 million in gifts and pledges.

The college used a combination of campaign money and the proceeds of the tax-exempt first-mortgage bonds to complete both renovation projects. One, a recreation center, added a new field house to a renovated gymnasium. It met important needs for physical education, athletics, and recreation. It also made the college more appealing to applicants for admission. The other added needed emphasis to humanities education. It sheltered the humanities departments in a carefully restored landmark, a turn-of-the-century Henry Hobson Richardson–style Romanesque revival classroom building.

Tax-exempt bonds represent one of a variety of borrowing options available. The tax-exempt feature enables a college or university to borrow at rates lower than those available in the regular financial markets. Baldwin-Wallace chose to combine the tax-exempt feature with a six-month floating rate rather than a fixed rate. The interest rate of each issue is adjusted by the bond trustee every six months. The college gained the initial benefit of lower short-term rates but also the risk involved in future rate fluctuations. To supplement the security provided by the mortgages on the facilities, B-W also chose to pay annual fees for underlying letters of credit from a large commercial bank. The effect is to substitute the bank's credit and reputation for that of the college, making the bonds more marketable at a lower interest rate. Other credit enhancement options that could have been used are credit insurance, guarantees, or issuance of added collateral.

Issuing tax-exempt bonds is a complicated process. In Ohio, Baldwin-Wallace needed preliminary and then final approval from a state agency. Then, bond counsel (paid by the college but representing the public), college counsel, the underwriter, independent auditors, and the letter-of-credit bank prepared an imposing stack of legal documents. The fixed issuance fees were substantial, and such fees must be considered along with the interest when evaluating the total cost of an issue.

Of course, debt requires future payments of principal and interest. Baldwin-Wallace has prepared a detailed repayment plan with several fund sources. The sources are payments of gift pledges from campaign donors, uses of capital gifts now temporarily invested, and annual mandatory transfers of unrestricted current funds. These transfers are already built into the budget. Any borrower must clearly demonstrate repayment capability, and this requirement limits the amount of debt that any institution can undertake. Federal and state laws impose legal limits, as well, on tax-exempt debt.

Using Enrollment and Admissions to Expand Resources

A characteristic common to the two institutions discussed is aggressive and effective recruiting of new students. Ohio Wesleyan was unwilling to accept the enrollment decline as permanent. In addition to adopting the measures already described, the university reorganized the admissions office and increased its budget. Baldwin-Wallace had also revamped its admissions procedures in the early 1980s and maintained a well-staffed and well-funded operation. The work of the admissions office was fundamental to Ohio Wesleyan's rebound and to Baldwin-Wallace's move to an all-time peak FTE enrollment.

This characteristic was rather common to much of higher education in the 1980s. Institutions generally have worked to preserve enrollment in the face of demographic trends. Responding to a survey (Hamlin and

Hungerford, 1988-1989), fifty-one college presidents who had actually dealt with financial crisis ranked thirty-nine factors for utility in overcoming such crises. The highest-ranked factor was expanded recruiting efforts, followed closely by better fund raising, better public relations, tuition hikes, and the addition or updating of programs. All of these steps ranked higher in the survey than program cuts and layoffs.

In late 1987, 380 private colleges and universities responded to a survey conducted jointly by the National Association of College and University Business Officers, the National Association of College Admissions Counselors, and the American Association of Collegiate Registrars and Admissions Officers. This survey was part of a study of admissions policies and related costs (National Association of College and University Business Officers, 1989). Seventy-one percent of the respondents reported receiving, over the previous five years, admissions budget increases proportionately greater than budget increases for other activities of the institution. Most of the remaining respondents had received increases proportionately equal to those for other activities. Sixty-one percent of the respondents were trying to increase the number of students, while virtually all claimed to be maintaining or improving academic quality.

The respondents were spending the new money covering wider geographic areas, targeting students of nontraditional college age, and using new or modified techniques. Items specifically mentioned included more glossy publications, search mailings, video cassettes, telephoning by faculty or student volunteers, organized campus visitations, advertising, and, as at Ohio Wesleyan, nonneed-based financial aid.

Summary

When admissions spending and emphasis achieve the desired results, colleges and universities can employ the added student revenue to build reserves and achieve specific objectives. Successful gift solicitation and the issuance of debt can provide funds for other goals, often endowment and plant. When enrollment does drop, by design or otherwise, careful program review can lead to responsible budget reductions.

References

Hamlin, A., and Hungerford, C. "How Private Colleges Survive a Financial Crisis: Tools for Effective Planning and Management." *Planning for Higher Education,* 1988-1989, *17* (2), 29-37.

Hyatt, J. A., Shulman, C. H., and Santiago, A. A. *Reallocation Strategies for Effective Resource Management.* Washington, D.C.: National Association of College and University Business Officers, 1984.

National Association of College and University Business Officers. *Assessing the Costs of Student Recruitment.* Washington, D.C.: National Association of College and University Business Officers, 1989.

Keith W. Mathews is vice-president for finance, Baldwin-Wallace College. Previously, he was controller at Ohio Wesleyan University.

Fragmentation of power within colleges and universities makes educational programs the element of higher education most resistant to organized change; yet, over time, persistent and thoughtful leadership can transform these programs.

Changing the Educational Program

Richard J. Wood

When I discuss curriculum with colleagues, whether members of the teaching faculty, deans, or presidents, I find them almost universally surprised that I as a president retain an active interest in the educational program. Then, when they learn that I am actually trying to influence its shape, many of them are incredulous. Many presidents, it seems, have given up any hope of changing the academic program, both because of other demands on their time and attention and because of its resistance to alteration.

Yet the academic programs of colleges and universities *do* change—in response to disciplinary and social pressures, in reply to changing faculty interests, in reaction sometimes to varying student interests and needs. What they do not tend to do is change in any coherent fashion that reflects the mission of the institution that houses them. My purpose in this chapter is not to analyze the reasons for resistance to change but to suggest strategies that can affect development toward greater coherence in educational programs. Coherence should be emphasized because curricular fragmentation is a pervasive problem in higher education, but in stressing coherence I do not exclude consideration of change to meet new challenges. The real question for American baccalaureate institutions is this: Will our response to the challenges facing us make any curricular sense, or will it simply add more academic dominoes to an unordered row?

To lend some concreteness to the conception of coherence in educational programs, I will highlight here some elements of my educational program agenda since assuming the presidency of Earlham College in Richmond, Indiana, in 1985. The following bear mention:

1. Creation of an agreed-on standard of quantitative literacy and mathematical skills to be required for all introductory science courses, followed

NEW DIRECTIONS FOR HIGHER EDUCATION, no. 71, Fall 1990 © Jossey-Bass Inc., Publishers by the development of sequences of science courses that build on and employ the required concepts and skills

2. Provision of a range of choices among ordered sets of courses in the social sciences (to replace the current random sampling), the completion of which will satisfy distribution requirements—these sets should, among other things, grant attention to global systems and problems

3. Expansion of the range of opportunities available for study abroad and arrangement of Earlham's curriculum so that all students, no matter what their major, can participate in study abroad and acquire high-level proficiency in a second language

4. Redirection of all foreign language instruction to proficiency-based teaching and testing and redefinition of the foreign language requirement for graduation so that all students attain levels of proficiency beyond those with which they began college

5. Improvement of the integration of on-campus with off-campus study.

After almost five years of effort, none of these goals has been achieved, but we have made some progress toward all five. In fairness to the faculty, I must note that I have not pressed for all of them every year, both because they have to become the faculty's goals and be shaped by the faculty if we are to succeed and because I have developed and am also pursuing many other goals outside the realm of educational programs. Still, change in the educational arena is harder to achieve than in any other (except perhaps that of student life). It is thus easy to become cynical about providing leadership for the kind of educational program change that I am seeking. Yet cynicism is always as self-defeating as it is self-justifying.

To undertake seriously the task of changing educational programs requires a substantial time commitment, stubbornness, and patience. Presidents and deans who stay in office only a few years or, even worse, who assume their positions with only a five-year horizon cannot expect to effect educational change.

This last point is obvious, but it is often lost. In dealing with topics such as educational change, we must begin with a return to the obvious. I suggest the following as leading elements of such a return.

Wood's Obvious Principles for Educational Change

Time. Change in educational programs will take longer than it should.

Leadership. Change in the direction of educational coherence requires faculty leadership, but the faculty will not provide that leadership without administrative leadership and support.

Cost. Change toward educational coherence will cost money. We take it for granted that new courses and new research projects will need funding. There is no reason to think that more fundamental educational change will be any different. What is different is that administrators will need to *initiate* funding for educational change, not simply respond to faculty demand.

Direction. Change toward educational coherence will not be achieved in a linear fashion or at a uniform pace. What is important, then, is to maintain the direction, to keep to the course.

Conversation. Change toward educational coherence will happen only if faculty members discuss educational issues with each other. The absence of such conversation virtually guarantees maintenance of the status quo.

Supporting Academic Entrepreneurship

There is another principle for educational change that seems to me to be no less obvious than those just discussed, although it probably requires some justification. This is the principle that change toward curricular coherence is more likely to occur in an environment in which educational innovation is also encouraged. Experimentation and diversity can coincide with—even support—the movement toward coherence, provided that administrative leadership does not lose sight of the larger goal of coherence.

Supporting Creativity. A former university president once described academic administration as being like the work of a gardener. The function of administration was to water (with money and encouragement) delicate shoots of new ideas. The kind of support for which I am calling should, however, be called the "beyond-the-watering-can model." Unless we add to the model of administration as a form of gardening the quality of selectivity in watering and even in weeding, this understanding of administration will indeed bring educational change, but the change will be random and perhaps quite at odds with the mission of the institution.

There is another important point about supporting creativity: The administration that does not support creativity that it does not originate will have a tough time getting faculty support for change that it wants. Besides, there is no reason to believe that administrators possess a monopoly of good ideas for educational programs or that only administrators can take an institution-wide view.

Embracing Unexpected Opportunities. Educational programs, like other products, need champions. Those champions must be found in the faculty if an innovation is to be profound and long-lasting. Administrators should not be shy about seeking out faculty champions. Nowhere is it written that we have to wait for them to emerge. But as we conduct the search for champions, it is important that we remain open to creative ideas that might, even if they are a bit oblique to our main purposes, come up unexpectedly and yet also further institutional goals. The move toward coherence cannot proceed along a straight line in a community as complex as a college or a university. Securing additional coherence will itself never be simple. New programs often open up unforeseen opportunities—for instance, by posing the possibility of seeing from a new perspective the relationships between existing programs and departments.

One of Earlham's most successful programs over the past fifteen years, Human Development and Social Relations, is a joint psychology and sociology venture. It has over time led to the development of new relationships between those departments and the departments of philosophy and religion. The growth of such programs as Japanese Studies has, in turn, affected Human Development and Social Relations through the creation of new offerings such as "The Family in Cross-Cultural Perspective."

It turns out, then, that serious efforts toward changing educational programs require provision of flexible, budgeted support for new programs and fund raising to support other people's ideas, as well as attempts to persuade those folks of the importance and wisdom of one's own ideas.

Creating Agreement for Change

The remainder of this chapter derives principles for changing educational programs on a larger scale—such as changing general education requirements—from a particular example that I lived through while serving as dean of the faculty at Whittier College in Whittier, California, from 1980 until 1985. (Those who have been reading carefully will have noted that I said that five years is too short a time to manage meaningful program change. Certainly, the *expectation* of a short term, which I did not entertain, would have inhibited the effort at Whittier, because when I assumed my position there the likelihood was high that the effort would take a long time. The readiness of the faculty to consider change permitted progress that was much more rapid than could reasonably have been expected.) I will recount what I take to be the essential steps that were followed and then illustrate them with brief accounts of the actual process at Whittier.

Agreeing on the Mission. The first step, the essential step, the "without which, nothing" step is to secure widespread agreement on the mission of the institution. Depending on the institution and the program, this agreement could be on the mission of the entire university or college, or that of a school, or even that of a department. Such an agreement does not guarantee that change will come, but it is a necessary precondition for successful innovation. Without such an agreement, change will not come.

When Eugene Mills became president of Whittier College in 1979, he recognized immediately that the institution lacked a common sense of mission. It had not decided whether to emphasize an identity as a high-quality, residential, undergraduate liberal arts college or an identity as a market-driven small university with an array of off-campus extension programs and of professional and graduate offerings. One of the first tasks that Mills undertook was to work with a group of faculty members to craft a new mission statement and to win its adoption by the faculty (unanimously!) during his first year in office. That mission statement played a role in my decision to go to Whittier, for it opted for excellence as a small, residential, high-quality liberal arts college. In subsequent years, we sharpened this mission and persuaded the board of trustees that it was right for Whittier.

Comparing the Present Program with Future Possibilities. Agreement on mission establishes the context for planning, which must proceed from a discussion comparing present programs with possible future curricula. If this conversation is to be fruitful for innovation, it will need to stir a widespread willingness to search for better alternatives to present programs. Parochialism and the relative isolation—should one say insularity?—of one college or university from others is a major obstacle to the development of openness to new ideas. The reluctance of many faculty members to consider that there might be useful lessons to be learned from the experiences of other institutions can be a particularly tricky problem. The feeling that "we" are so unique that we have nothing to learn from other colleges or universities is death to change.

Given the obstacles to be overcome, the discussion of alternatives may take several years. It can often be facilitated through recourse to the services of an outside consultant, who is preferably a colleague from a similar institution. The consultancy program of the National Endowment for the Humanities (NEH) has been an especially helpful mechanism for many institutions.

The faculty leadership at Whittier had agreed in 1980 on the main features of the college's mission. They also believed that the general education curriculum of the college did not adequately reflect this mission or the actual quality of the institution.

By the time I assumed my position at Whittier, the faculty leadership had applied for and received an NEH consultancy grant. They had also identified a consultant, Professor Daniel Horowitz from Scripps College. We began soon to identify areas of the curriculum in which greater coherence might be achieved and to look for institutions that might be relevant models.

Appointing Choice Makers. The third step in improving the climate for innovation is the appointment of a respected group of faculty members and administrators to begin to choose among the options available. Who serves in this group is fundamental to its chances for success. It is important to be sensitive to campus politics in determining the composition of the group and not to let a flawed selection process produce a weak group. But *who* serves is much more important than *how* the selection is made. The process of appointment will be attacked, in any case, by those who do not like the choices. It will be ignored by those who like them.

Providing Administrative Support. Provision of administrative support for the faculty-dominated, choice-making group is the essential fourth step to securing change. Members of the group need to know that administrators think that what they are doing is important, and they need to have the time to do it well. Clerical and computing support and released time for the faculty participants are often helpful, as are opportunities to visit other institutions known to offer relevant alternative programs.

At Whittier, the group working with the consultant became the nucleus of a planning committee. The faculty executive committee had approved its membership, so there were no process issues concerning the choice of those selected to serve. Both the associate academic dean and I served on it. Not all of the group's members were senior faculty, but all were highly respected.

The NEH grant supported visits by faculty teams to several other institutions. As we made progress, it became clear that a sustained opportunity to work together would be beneficial, so the president and I released the faculty members of the committee from their January term teaching obligations in order to devote full time to curriculum planning. Thus, by the early spring of 1982 we had drafted an outline plan.

Remaining Focused on the Objective. It is imperative to hold to a clear sense of priorities in working toward innovation. The faculty committee will want and need to consider how global a program change needs to be. Change should be no bigger than is necessary to achieve the desired goal, both to avoid throwing out the baby with the bath and to get the program adopted. The relevant political principle here is this: Do not fight unnecessary battles. Many a good idea for educational program innovation is lost because it becomes linked with an unpopular idea that is essentially irrelevant to the good idea's implementation.

There were several areas in which we might have sought curricular reform at Whittier, but the planning committee decided to suggest only minor reforms in the natural science requirement portion of our distribution requirements and to concentrate, instead, on the social sciences, the arts, and the humanities. Some members wanted to try to change the way that English composition was handled, but it became clear that this issue was too sensitive politically. To tackle it would have jeopardized the entire reform effort. (The composition program was finally changed in 1985 and 1986.) The departments that the proposed innovations would most directly affect were the college's strongest and most confident, so there was considerable openness to change. The most important element of the proposal was the replacement of an unstructured set of distribution options with carefully planned pairs of courses, thematically related and drawn from two disciplines. Under the emerging plan, development of such pairs would be the only way that departments could secure approval of their courses to satisfy general education requirements.

Engaging in Widespread Consultation. The sixth step toward change comes when the planning group begins to move toward a proposal. This step involves engaging in widespread consultation, preferably through the use of small groups. Consultation should occur first with the individuals whom the proposal will most affect, then with those whom it will not greatly affect but whose support is needed in order to gain approval. This latter group is often neglected, but opposition from it can stop change.

In the early part of the spring semester in 1982, the planning group published a preliminary draft proposal. The planners divided into teams in order to meet with small groups of faculty members, usually convened along departmental lines, to discuss the proposed changes. All who were involved in this process are convinced that this step was crucial for improving the ideas under consideration, for lowering anxieties, and for building a consensus for reform.

Revising in Response to Suggestions. If the planning committee is good, it will learn from the consultations and will make revisions in the proposal that will be widely seen as improving it. After doing so, the committee is probably at the point where it is ready to seek formal approval for the plan and begin implementation.

Whittier's planning group listened during the consultation stage of the process and incorporated revisions into the proposal. When the proposed new liberal education curriculum underwent formal consideration at a faculty meeting, it won approval, without dissent, in a single session. Subsequently, the program attracted significant funding from NEH and from the Fund for the Improvement of Postsecondary Education. The revised general education plan continues to be the heart of Whittier College's curriculum.

Establishing Managerial Support. Implementation of a major program change needs to become someone's responsibility. A committee can exercise oversight, but committees do a poor job of *managing* implementation. Just as committees can edit but not write, so committees can oversee but not implement. Too often, administrations fail to provide the time and attention needed to ensure effective efforts to bring a new program into operation. I am speaking here not so much about arranging for members of the administration to endorse and offer budgetary support for the program as I am about making provision for someone to give it direct, sustained oversight—in short, to manage it.

At Whittier, we placed one of the champions of the new general education curriculum, a part-time associate academic dean, in charge of carrying it into effect. He worked with a faculty committee whose members were also champions of the program. Because of the structure of the new curriculum, new pairs of courses must be developed each year. Hence, continuing managerial attention is necessary to ensure that the needed courses are designed, scheduled, and taught.

Conclusion

The eight steps pursued at Whittier College, although they were associated with a particular instance of academic program innovation, work generally. When I think of other program changes in which I was involved as a faculty member, the successful ones all followed the process outlined, albeit sometimes more informally.

The educational program agenda that I sketched for Earlham College earlier in this chapter cannot be accomplished through a single iteration of the change process. Realizing all of the goals set out or something resembling them will require several separate efforts. One is under way as I write. A task force on global education is in place, with responsibility for planning and coordinating changes in study abroad, in language study, and in the integration of on- and off-campus study and for finding a way to pay attention in the curriculum to global systems. It is too early to predict success, but the ingredients are there, and success is likely if the principles and process set out here are followed.

Richard J. Wood, former dean of the faculty at Whittier College, is president of Earlham College.

Adapting faculty personnel policies through creation or revision of a faculty handbook may respond constructively to change or, more important, may serve as a catalyst for change that extends to programs, administrative organization, and even the campus culture.

Adapting Faculty Personnel Policies

James L. Pence

Colleges and universities rarely revise faculty personnel policies without some stimulus. Challenges to interpretations of specific provisions, discoveries of omissions, or the arrival of a new president are common stimuli. Major changes in institutional strategy, such as those resulting from programmatic redirection or administrative reorganization, usually prompt substantive alterations in personnel policies. Yet faculty policy manuals and handbooks do not typically receive regular reviews.

Based on the experiences of several campuses and especially on the experiences of the University of Southern Colorado where faculty handbook revision ended years of internal conflict, this chapter offers practical advice. It describes a model procedure for institutions undertaking revision projects in response to some stimulus and for institutional leaders contemplating strategic shifts in organizational direction. The process of revising faculty personnel policies can itself become the stimulus for change, enhancing opportunities for successful programmatic redirection or administrative reorganization.

The Faculty Handbook as a Living Policy Document

The task of adapting or revising faculty personnel policies is sometimes seen as a thankless job to be performed by personnel officers, executive secretaries, or administrative assistants who are responsible for accurately encoding institutional rules and regulations. This view fails to acknowledge the relationship between language and reality. Personnel policies shape the reality of the working lives of the faculty, who thus have a vested interest in

NEW DIRECTIONS FOR HIGHER EDUCATION, no. 71, Fall 1990 © Jossey-Bass Inc., Publishers   59 both their composition and their revision. Administrators entrusting the revision process to support staff are likely to encounter significant opposition from the faculty—as well they should!

The act of revising personnel policies should be seen by administrators and faculty alike as a collaborative writing project performed by institutional ethnographers who are creating or recreating the "story" the institution tells itself about itself. Much more than a collection of rules and regulations governing behavior, personnel policies constitute the institution's written account of its nature and character.

On most campuses, for example, faculty handbook passages dealing with tenure and promotion are seen as "sacred texts." Even minor modifications to key handbook sections are treated seriously by faculty members, especially if those modifications are proposed by administrators. A senior faculty member renowned for his authorship of a reduction-in-force policy may become a kind of Moses figure; changes to "his" policy are perceived as attempts to discredit him. A policy describing annual performance evaluation, no matter how badly in need of revision, will be defended on the floor of the faculty senate for its historical value.

Administrators holding this "literary" view of the policy revision process are likely to receive the endorsement and cooperation of the faculty. If the effort to adapt personnel policies becomes a tool for learning about the institution, planning for its future, clarifying its present, and contextualizing its past, it can become a catalyst for or the appropriate response to institutional change. The preferred outcome of a revision project is the production of a "living" policy document representing the nature and character of the institution as seen by its inscribers and ultimately sanctioned by its leaders and governors.

Necessity of Consultative Strategies

Institutions that are adapting faculty personnel policies to changing conditions or are revising policies to initiate a climate receptive to change have a greater chance of success if they operate with the literary view. However, adopting a new metaphor will not alone suffice. Institutional leaders must also consciously decide to employ consultative strategies within a process-oriented methodology to produce a living policy document.

The benefits and liabilities of consultation and participatory decision making in higher education are widely documented. In the case of adapting personnel policies, the members of the institutional team assigned the responsibility for revision must know from the outset that their collaboration will be respected as both process and product. Communicating this respect is the job of key administrators, especially the president. A commitment from the top to consultation, starting at the beginning of the project, is a prerequisite for success.

Interpretive Contexts. The team must also be fully aware of the three important interpretive contexts that faculty members bring to discussions of personnel policies. First, faculties see their campuses as workplaces. Employment conditions, workload issues, reward systems, and professional development opportunities are among their critical concerns. Second, faculty members see their campuses as organizations. Issues of communication, information flow, administrative organization, hierarchy, and bureaucracy will draw their attention throughout the revision process. Third, many faculty members regard their campus communities as cultures. For them, the important considerations of values, traditions, and symbols are relevant to all activities, and they will view policy revision in terms of impact on the institutional culture.

Advance Discussion. Institution leaders from the administration and the faculty should discuss these interpretive contexts before beginning the revision process. This discussion will yield important conclusions about organizational readiness to accommodate revisions to existing personnel policies. Plunging into the task without this kind of discussion will probably result in a technically proficient but not fully satisfactory document, just as an accomplished writer who fails to engage in suitable prewriting activities typically produces a competent but uninspired text.

Dividends of This Process. Collaborative writing projects require tremendous investments of resources, including especially the time of the participants and the ongoing support of those who commission the project. By adopting the literary metaphor, committing to consultation and a process orientation, and thinking about the interpretive contexts before beginning the revision process, institutional leaders can secure greater assurance than they otherwise would that the investment of resources will pay meaningful dividends. Few campuses in America can afford to waste valuable resources on projects not designed to yield fully satisfying results.

Eight-Stage Revision Process

The process of revising or adapting faculty personnel policies in institutions responding to or initiating change is conveniently described in eight separate stages.

Stage One: Establishing the Team. The first order of business is the establishment of a team charged with drafting the new or adapted policy document. The use of the team approach is especially important if the revision project will serve as the catalyst for other changes, because faculty members and administrators must learn to work together cooperatively for meaningful institutional change to occur. Since the team will be required to function as a collaborative writing group, its members should be chosen with care.

Preliminary Decisions. Before the team is constituted, administrative and faculty leaders must reach agreement on several key matters. These include criteria for selecting team members, qualities that these members should possess, and the rules under which they will operate.

Ideally the presidents of the institution and of the faculty governing body should collaborate on the decisions about criteria, qualities, and rules. Administrative collaboration with elected faculty representatives will signal clearly that the process of revising personnel policies will advance in an orderly fashion and will culminate in a document developed jointly by faculty and administrative team members. Many revision projects are endangered by the president's unilateral appointment of an ad hoc group, no matter how well regarded the appointees may be. If the faculty's leadership are involved from the beginning of the process, the team's final recommendations are less likely to be criticized as the work of the administration, and the team's faculty members will be able to participate knowing that they have received the endorsement of their own leaders.

Criteria for Selecting Team Members. The criteria to be used in the selection of team members will vary in accordance with campus cultures and governance practices. At the least it will be essential to consider, in the selection of both faculty and administrative members, whether they will be elected or appointed, how and by whom they will be chosen, under whose jurisdiction they will function, whether they will serve as representatives of their units or as individuals, and how many of each group will be chosen. It is important that the presidents agree on criteria to be applied to both groups so that the faculty perceive that their leadership has as much say as the administration in the constitution of the team. It is crucial that the number of faculty members on the team exceeds the number of administrators so that the faculty know that they possess the majority vote. The size of the team will vary according to the scope of the project, but a team of seven voting members (at least four of whom are faculty members) is usually sufficient. The presidents should consider adding a nonvoting recording secretary or clerk to the team. This person convenes the team, records its decisions, and handles details associated with the preparation of drafts. She or he should be either an academic administrator or a faculty member who has credibility with team members and the larger campus community.

Personal Qualities. Similarly, agreement should be reached on the personal qualities desired in members of the team. Common examples include an ability to rise above "turf" issues, a capacity to maintain a task orientation, a willingness to remain open and flexible in the process of exchanging ideas, an ability to write, a knowledge of the institution (including the organizational saga), a preference for a problem-solving orientation toward institutional challenges, and an ability to work in a group as a member of a team. Agreeing on the desired qualities will not always ensure success, but the act of reaching agreement should precipitate the selection of a team predisposed to collaboration.

Rules of Order. Finally, the presidents should agree on the rules of order under which the team will operate, if they wish to prescribe rules prior to the team's selection. Imposing rules on a team after it is organized and working will impede progress. If the presidents wish to delegate to the team responsibility for designing its own operating procedures, they should agree to such delegation from the beginning. Among rules of order to be discussed are voting rules (when to take votes, who votes, how votes are recorded); team requirements for confidentiality; reporting relationship of the team to the presidents; what constitutes a quorum; and whether the team will have a leader, will choose its own chair, and how the chair functions. Given the collaborative nature of this kind of project, many campuses find that teams work best without votes and without a formally designated chair. To protect the integrity of the process, confidentiality is best maintained until the document is ready for distribution. In any event, rules must be designed, whether by the presidents or by the team, to encourage cooperation, collaboration, and consensus building.

Team Selection and Communication of the Charge. After the important preliminary decisions have been made, this stage of the revision process enters a second phase during which team members are selected and receive a charge. After team members have been chosen, the presidents should jointly convene a meeting at which to present the formal charge. For symbolic and substantive reasons, the members of the team must perceive that their charge is the result of planning, discussing, and negotiating between the faculty and administrative leadership. This perception will give team members a clear understanding of their mandate at the outset of their work.

Notification. The first stage ends with notification of the entire campus community of the membership of the team, its charge, and the expected outcome. If everyone on campus knows what is happening, who is involved, and what is expected, the revision process will not be shrouded in secrecy, although the work of the team is confidential. A memorandum jointly signed by the presidents will often suffice as suitable notification.

Use of Consultants. Institutional leaders should also decide on the use of consultants in the revision process. Frequently, handbook specialists who understand legal, political, and technical issues in higher education can provide valuable assistance to the institutional team. A key consideration in the decision to use consultants is the availability of suitable expertise on campus. Smaller institutions frequently discover that consultants can provide the objectivity necessary to guide the process. Likewise, institutions whose handbooks have not yet been reviewed in the light of recent legal developments affecting higher education are well advised to consider employing outside assistance. Finally, some colleges find themselves unable to marshal the internal human resources necessary to initiate and monitor the project. Consultants can serve the useful function of keeping the project moving to completion. If consultants are used, the presidents should specify and communicate to the team what the consultants' responsibilities will be.

Stage Two: Initializing the Team. During this stage, the team plans how to carry out its assigned charge. Key decisions include determination of scope, identification of issues, and assignment of specific tasks to team members.

Determination of the Scope of Revision. Questions of scope arise early in any project involving the revision of faculty personnel policies. Does the team, for example, have license to include new policies in the final document, or is it restricted to revisions of existing policies? Can it recommend deletion of existing provisions, or is it bound to stay within certain limits? If the charge to the group does not specify scope, the team must make a quick determination of its full responsibilities.

It is a helpful strategy for the team to collect and categorize existing personnel policies, including those that are officially a part of the institution's manual and those that are "fugitives." On many campuses, fugitive policies exist in files of department chairs or in notebooks compiled by administrative officers; these are the policies that are known to be functional but that have no official status.

Another useful strategy is to compare the existing personnel manual with the manuals of comparable institutions or with outlines intended to serve as a guide for the composition of policy documents. In the case of faculty handbooks, the outline prepared by Thomas Emmet and published in the *Chronicle of Higher Education* ("Writing a Faculty Handbook," 1985) is widely used.

Identification of the Issues. The identification of issues to be resolved frequently results from the determination of scope, especially as the team comes to perceive that specific policies must be added to or deleted from the existing manual. At this point, the team must carefully delineate the issues that are likely to affect their work.

For example, an analysis of the Emmet outline may yield the discovery that the institution has no policy covering the use of software. Perhaps at issue is the role of the computer science department in designing such a policy. The team may decide to consult with the department's chair prior to designing a policy, thus setting a precedent for consultation in the drafting of other needed new policies. Clearly, the specific determination of an omission has in this example resulted in the identification of a seminal issue that the team is well advised to resolve before proceeding further.

Assignment of Tasks. When scope and issues to be resolved have been determined, team members should be assigned specific tasks and target dates for completion of preliminary drafts. One method often used in making such assignments is to categorize policies according to common themes. For example, one subgroup of the team could be assigned to work on all policies related to legal or contractual issues, another to performance assessment, and a third to salary and benefits. Another method is to divide the team into groups according to functions: a group to recommend deletions, a group to recommend additions, and one to survey needed revisions.

Before the process moves to the third stage, team members must possess a clear understanding of the scope of their work, the issues that they must address, and their individual responsibilities to the group. When such understandings exist, the entire process is expedited.

Stage Three: Drafting the Policies. Working in subgroups, team members compose sections of the policy manual, reformatting existing policies, writing new ones, or discovering rationale for the elimination of others. Since everyone understands that the challenge is to prepare drafts, no one needs to be concerned that what is produced at this stage is forever cast in stone.

Principles of Composition. Prior to beginning drafts, team members need to agree on certain principles of composition. For example, they should discuss topics of style, usage, syntax, and mechanics. Coming from a variety of disciplinary contexts, team members will undoubtedly bring differing linguistic preferences to their work as composers. Therefore, agreeing in advance on matters of language is an important step in the process.

Group Exercises. One useful device is to conduct a case study on precatory language, and how to avoid it, with the goal of sensitizing team members to the problems in interpretation sure to result, for example, from the use of "should" when "will" is really intended. As writers of policy, they need to be reminded that clarity, brevity, and concision are virtues. Another device is to engage in a group activity of analyzing policy language, choosing an effective model to guide individual writers as they prepare drafts. Reaching consensus on matters of language is an important task in the third stage, if for no other reason than to expedite the process in stage four.

Stage Four: Revising and Editing the Policies. There are many possible approaches to revising and editing the texts that the subcommittees write: For example, a special new subcommittee can be assigned this task; an individual committee member can complete it; the recording secretary can take it on; an individual faculty member or administrator can perform it; or the entire handbook committee can accomplish it.

Committee of the Whole. The preferred method is for the team to work as a committee of the whole. Each group should circulate a manuscript of its text to the other team members prior to the first meeting dedicated to group editing. The subgroup should enjoy an opportunity to make an oral presentation of its work, giving group members a chance to explain reasons for doing what they have done. Following the oral presentation, the entire team works patiently through the text, editing, building consensus on specific passages, and gaining confidence in team members' abilities to work together. Continuing in this manner, the team completes a working draft of the policies under consideration. It is this draft that becomes the document that is circulated in stage five.

Recording Secretary. If a recording secretary was not originally selected for the project, it is useful at this point for the team to identify one of its members whose sole responsibility is to keep track of group decisions on the text. This person must take care not to interject anything of his or her persona into the content; the secretary's duty is to produce a clean text faithfully based on the group's consensus. On occasion, the secretary may translate the group's thinking into draft language for review at a later date, provided that the secretary writes well and enjoys the trust of the entire team.

At the conclusion of this stage, the working draft must be readied for circulation to those affected by the revision process, and it is crucial that the document that goes out to the campus community accurately reflects the collective wisdom and the unified consensus of the team.

Stage Five: Authenticating the Draft. It is at this critical stage of the process that the team's working draft, held so far in confidence, is circulated to the community for its reaction. The procedure employed to seek authentication is crucial to the success of the project, for the way in which the document is presented may have as much impact on the campus community as do the document's contents.

Usefulness of Hearings. Campus culture and historical precedent will probably inform the direction of the process in the fifth stage. One common approach is for the team to hold open hearings with faculty groups, where it receives written and oral testimony on the working draft. Provided that all affected faculty units are given the opportunity to testify, hearings may be the most efficient and effective approach to seeking authentication. Obviously, the team must be prepared at this stage to listen critically to comments offered by colleagues who, for the most part, know less about the subjects contained in the document than the team members do. The ability of the team to respond maturely to these hearings will undoubtedly influence the successful completion of the project. A team responding defensively will have a more difficult task completing the project than a team responding with genuine interest in making the draft better, which could mean making it more acceptable to the various constituencies on campus.

Response to Substantive Comments. It is important for the team to record, discuss, and respond to every substantive comment received from colleagues. It may be that, on serious reflection on the testimony given by the English department, for example, the team will decide not to modify the document to conform to that department's ideas. It behooves the team, in this case, to demonstrate to their English colleagues that the department's ideas were considered but not incorporated for specific reasons. If the team is not serious about using ideas from the community, holding hearings is a waste of time; conversely, if the team takes every idea that it hears in testimony, the project completion date will be unnecessarily extended. The team must demonstrate beyond doubt that it listens, evaluates critically, and decides fairly in response to campus hearings. Otherwise, the document will not be authenticated, although it may subsequently be approved.

Helpfulness of Presidential Involvement. At this point in the process, some campuses decide to authenticate the document by inviting the presidents to exercise a "dotted-line relationship" with the team, offering their comments and criticisms. If the goal of the authentication stage is to build the consensus needed to win approval for the document, the presidents can provide valuable assistance. The institutional president, for example, can alert the team to potential problems with the governing board, and the faculty president can speak to political obstacles to approval. In a true collaboration, faculty members and administrators are partners in the enterprise. This is the time for negotiation, before the document is finalized for approval.

If consultants have been involved in the work of the team, they can serve a useful function in the authentication process by helping the team in its deliberations. Consultants are less likely than team members to hold pride of authorship in the policy document and will be able to evaluate impartially the merit of comments and criticisms coming out of the hearings. Consultants can also be helpful to the presidents, alerting them to potential obstacles to final approval.

Stage Six: Approving the Final Document. When the working draft of the document is completely revised in accordance with the team's evaluation of comments directed to it in stage five, it should be prepared for the approval process. If the changes are to be sent to the faculty in a referendum, the approval procedure will likely follow the prescriptions of existing policy governing faculty votes. If the changes are to be considered by the representative body of the faculty, its rules will govern the approval process.

Regardless of the procedures used, the final document approved by internal constituencies should be the one sent to the governing board for external endorsement. In rare instances, the institutional president may make minor revisions in the document approved internally; the ideal situation is for the presidents to endorse jointly the internally approved document. A governing board faced with a policy document jointly endorsed by the faculty and the administration is likely to be receptive to its contents and supportive of the collaborative process used to generate it.

Stage Seven: Implementing Change. Massive restructuring of policy documents almost always means changing the way that institutions do business. Even minor revisions in faculty personnel policies can necessitate major procedural changes. Institutions emerging from the revision process with an approved policy document are wise to consider the effects of administering the new document. Implementation contains several requirements.

First, institutional leadership must ensure that all affected parties receive complete and accurate copies of modified policies. Second, new policies must be explained to those responsible for administering them, and appropriate staff development activities must be planned and executed. Finally, a responsible individual or office must be assigned the duty of monitoring implementation and informing the presidents of problems. Without taking care in the implementation stage, institutions may find that the hard work of revision or adaptation fails to pay the expected dividends.

Stage Eight: Evaluating and Celebrating Change. Given the investment of time and energy in the revision of personnel policies, institutions must hold themselves accountable for evaluation of the outcomes of the revision process. Periodically, faculty and administrative leadership should assess the extent to which policy revisions have made an impact on the lives of people in the institution. If revisions unwittingly result in generally perceived negative impacts, the remedy is to "do it over." If adaptations produce positive outcomes, those outcomes should be celebrated. It is likewise important to celebrate the accomplishments of the team. The presidents may host a dinner or reception to thank team members for their contributions, and the campus community should be reminded of the benefits resulting from collaboration. Affirming the process is perhaps more important than touting the product in those institutions where collaboration has been rarely effective or seldom used.

Conclusion

The final impact of adapting faculty personnel policies to reply to or to induce institutional change can be measured in terms of the extent to which those adaptations are perceived by faculty and administration as successful. The real benefit of undertaking a revision project to encourage institutional change is ultimately evaluated in terms of the changes that such a project brings about. The worth of a revision to meet change lies in its effectiveness as a response. Continuous evaluation of the product and the process calls to the attention of the entire community the outcomes of the revision process and may provide community members with just cause to celebrate their accomplishment in replying to or initiating meaningful change.

Reference

"Writing a Faculty Handbook: A Two-Year, Nose-to-the-Grindstone Process." *Chronicle of Higher Education*, 1985, *31* (5), 28.

James L. Pence is vice-president for academic affairs at Wartburg College, Waverley, Iowa, and is an expert on faculty handbooks.

Changing priorities in corporate and foundation giving—and, in some cases, in individual philanthropy—pose new challenges and create new opportunities for college and university leaders seeking new sources of external funding.

Developing New Contributor Constituencies

Helmut Hofmann

The decade of the 1980s witnessed significant shifts in the philanthropic priorities of corporate, foundation, and many individual contributors that have long provided important external funding for institutions of higher education. Among the foremost of these shifts are a growing tendency to direct gifts toward sharply defined goals set by the contributors, an increasing concern to respond to the needs of new recipient groups outside of the college and university community, and a rising desire to hold the beneficiaries of charitable gifts accountable for their expenditures and to target for gift support those who are demonstrably most effective at managing gifts to achieve desired ends. Larger and, in most instances, better qualified professional staffs have become fixtures in contributors' chambers and administer available funds through the application of clearly defined giving criteria and of well-developed and specific procedural guidelines.

Institutional development or advancement teams in colleges and universities, as well as in other fund-raising entities, must reply to these changed conditions with a full understanding of the challenges and the opportunities that they pose. Both a business-as-usual attitude and a hope for the return of the golden age of unrestricted giving of funds must be and are being abandoned as relics of a lost—and probably irrecoverable—past. In their place must come a realistic grasp of prevailing giving priorities in the changed philanthropic environment; this knowledge is an absolute essential for any successful attempt to develop new contributor constituencies and new sources of outside funding for institutions of higher learning. For example, if an organization or individual previously known for unrestricted giving has embraced "focused" giving as a guiding principle, then approaches to this source of gifts must change accordingly, from the customary contact soliciting unrestricted funds to contacts responsive to the new emphasis. If givers have established "targeted" contributions as the governing priority, then institutions seeking funds from them must frame their requests appropriately. In other words, an institution must demonstrate both that its use of the funds will be effective enough to warrant its being targeted as a recipient and that this use will serve the specific philanthropic objectives of the giver. For example, if funding sources have adopted particular goals in response to identified social concerns, a college or university seeking contributions must fashion relevant institutional linkages to such concerns before approaching those funding sources. What all of this means is that the successful identification, cultivation, and solicitation of new outside funding sources, in particular of new corporate and foundation funding sources, require thorough preparation. There must be careful research into donor interests, into donor procedural and policy guidelines, and into ways that institutional goals and needs must be adapted to these interests and guidelines if there is to be a successful approach for support.

Preparing to Make Requests

Inventory Needs. In order to match a college or university's funding needs with the philanthropic interests of prospective new contributors, the institutional advancement team (president, trustees, development officers, and relevant deans and faculty members) must first prepare detailed inventories of those funding needs. It is desirable to prioritize these needs and to draft a statement about their relationships to short- and long-range institutional plans. Potential donors frequently ask for information about these relationships, and they prefer to review well-prepared proposals that have resulted from comprehensive institutional planning efforts rather than from hastily written responses to requests for proposals.

Budget Conservatively. Authors of funding requests should heed this caution: They should always write budget requests that are conservative, realistic, and defensible. The strategy of shooting for large sums in the hope of receiving at least a portion of the amount requested is a poor one. Individual contributors and foundation and corporate giving officers are far more likely to respond favorably to conservatively conceived proposals.

Match Contributors' Funding Cycles. It is also important to recognize that requests for funding commitments that extend beyond a period of two years or so exceed the funding cycles of most institutional givers. Colleges and universities should therefore incorporate into proposals for funding long-term projects a provision for internal funding to follow the initial phase for which outside support is sought. In this context, academic administrators may find it necessary to restrain overly ambitious proposal writers, whose combined funding requests can tend to outpace the grant-making capacity of a given contributor and can therefore oblige a college or university to add substantially to its own expenditures when the outside funding expires.

Consider a Joint Proposal. Inventorying institutional funding needs, articulating relationships between funding needs and short- and long-term goals, and budgeting realistically are the three steps initially required in any promising effort to develop new contributor constituencies and new sources of external funding. Smaller colleges and universities are well advised to consider an additional step: preparation of proposals jointly with other institutions.

Joint ventures and joint proposals can carry significant advantages. One such advantage is that the combining of efforts can add depth and strength to a proposal from an institution whose own faculty and administrative personnel, stretched to the limit by heavy workloads, could not credibly undertake the project by themselves. Another advantage is that collaboration can be an important indication of institutional commitment to a venture, while promising as well to overcome the limitations that accompany geographic isolation. Cooperation can also promise increased impact from funding and may prove especially helpful where potential contributors are hesitant to support the projects of smaller institutions or of institutions set in regions of sparse population. Requests for support that rest on solid efforts of colleges and universities to pool their own resources and to subordinate their individual desires to larger common goals may generate the extra margin of interest that means contributor approval in instances when contributors are confronted with large numbers of strong competing proposals.

Be Specific About Objectives. In preparing institutional or cooperative inventories of funding needs, advancement teams are wise to avoid terms that do not convey specific meaning. Most potential givers have listened to too many applicants for funds who speak of the "value of a liberal education," "the unique mission of the institution," or "the commitment of a dedicated faculty." Such vague generalities may evoke clear images for a college or university's own constituency, but they do not suffice for potential new contributors, who are apt to want a specific and pithy characterization of an institution and its funding objectives.

Build on Existing Strengths. The final element in the preparatory stage is the completion of an impartial assessment of the existing internal strengths of the institution. The results of this evaluation provide the best foundation on which a funding effort can be built. Reviewers of requests for gifts find in existing strengths a much more compelling incentive for support than they find in a long list of weaknesses that a proposal for funding aims to remedy.

Searching for New Contributors

Make a Continuous Effort. A search for new contributors cannot be limited to a single, brief expenditure of resources and of staff time. It will require continuous attention to the changing priorities and funding goals of corporations, foundations, and individual givers in order to succeed. Institutional advancement officers must remain current in their knowledge of potential sources of funding. The best way to remain current is by making periodic inquiries at corporate or foundation contribution offices and by maintaining periodic personal association with individual donor prospects. At the least, advancement officers need to know the answers to four questions.

1. *Who Is in Charge?* Addressing the director of a contribution program or an individual donor prospect correctly is a matter of common courtesy, but it is also much more. The use of the correct name and mode of address increases the chance that an application will be read by the right person, rather than lost somewhere in the maze of postal delivery systems in large organizations. It also avoids the risk of inadvertently offending an addressee and heightens a reader's confidence that the advancement officer has prepared carefully in developing a proposal.

2. *What Are Funding Priorities?* A simple letter of inquiry or a conversation in person or by telephone will usually yield this information. Using it will help ensure that applications for support match the interests of potential contributors.

3. *When Must Proposals Be Submitted?* Most grantors operate according to established schedules with specified application deadlines. To apply without knowledge of due dates is to risk losing consideration because of a late or out-of-phase submission. Ordinarily the requested information will be forthcoming in response to a direct question about funding and application cycles.

4. *Which Approach Is Preferable?* Some grantors offer little or no direction concerning the shape of a written proposal. Others prescribe the use of application forms or the provision of specified information. Some even respond to oral approaches, especially if a personal relationship between applicant and donor has been established. Whatever the case, it is vital to know what form a request for support is to take. It is also vital to follow two cardinal rules. The first, unless a longer submission is expected, is to be brief and to concentrate the presentation in one or two sharply focused pages. Among other things, this narrative should provide a concise introduction to the applying institution. Staff members of philanthropists are usually quite busy, with only limited time to review applications. The second rule, when the initial presentation is to be made in an interview or when the applicant is invited to an interview, is to use the allotted time to best advantage. One should avoid making trivial conversation and come quickly

to the point. The old anecdote about the "elevator speech" may apply here: The interviewee should condense the presentation so that it could be made effectively on an elevator traveling between two consecutive floors.

It is a great advantage to gain an interview with a philanthropist or relevant staff member even before submitting a proposal. A conversation with a potential giver typically provides more information about the conduct of a contribution program than does study of printed guidelines. More important, since philanthropic gifts are made primarily to people rather than to institutions, direct conversation may begin to build or add to the foundation of trust underlying decisions to give. Either way, one improves the prospects for success in a request for funds.

Repeat Efforts. Informed properly about potential new donors, college and university advancement officers are ready to begin to develop new contributor constituencies. Even so, success will not normally be immediate. Those who charge officers to develop new giving constituencies must remember that potential new sources of external funding rarely respond with a yes to the first request for support. It is much more likely that the prospective grantor will reply with a no or a series of no's over a period of time before offering the first yes. The cultivation of new supporters will always remain a difficult, at times tedious, process. The task of identifying and courting them is not a task for the impatient. Good preparatory work, however, increases the likelihood of success. Diligent searching and basic industry, rather than genius or flashy proposals, are the best route to success.

Avoid Premature Announcements. An additional word of caution is advisable. Institutional officers must remember that a grant is never granted, a gift never given, until a check or at least a written notification of approval has arrived at the proper office of the college or university. One can avert major embarrassments by restraining eager personnel at all levels from publicizing grants before the final decisions have actually been made. Even after the decisions have been made, it is the course of courtesy and discretion to seek permission from grantors before publishing word of the happy event.

Making an Effective Case

Representatives of institutions seeking funds frequently meet with difficult questions. They are asked, "Why should we support your institution?" or "What will this gift do for us and for our image in the community?" or "How will you publicize this grant to your own constituency?" among other queries. The intent in asking is not to put fund raisers on the spot or to catch them off guard. Instead, these questions express the genuine concerns of many contributors. Why, indeed, should support be provided for a college or university when an obvious relationship between giver and recipient does not exist—or, equally important, when this relationship does not exist in the mind of the person who must approve the gift?

Those who must explain why support should be provided must furnish concise, specific, and pointed reasons. Recourse to stock phrases such as "corporate social responsibility" or "being a good corporate citizen and neighbor" are more likely to put off than to win support. After all, the overwhelming majority of philanthropically inclined corporations, foundations, and individuals are already good citizens and good neighbors. They care about the communities in which they reside or conduct business. They also know these things about themselves.

There are several proven, specific strategies for meeting the legitimate concerns of and establishing relationships with potential new contributors. The most useful follow.

Find an Alumni Connection to the Prospect. The possession of current and accurate information about the names, responsibilities, and number of alumni whom a prospective contributor employs often enables a vital first step in establishing a college's or a university's importance to the prospect. An institution able to demonstrate that its academic programs prepare a stream of talented and valued personnel is equipped to argue its importance to the potential giver in concrete and often persuasive terms. It is thus imperative to maintain adequate and up-to-date alumni records.

Point Out Employee Connections to the Institution. Information about the active participation of prospects' employees or associates in the affairs of a college or university can be similarly valuable. Current rosters of an institution's governing, advisory, alumni, and other boards and of its volunteer workers are invaluable. To be armed with this information is to enjoy a powerful advantage in dealing with potential sources of external funding.

Establish an Institutional Connection to the Contributor. The best approach, of course, is to create a direct relationship between the institution and the prospective grantor. There is no substitute for personal relationships between applicants for funds or their officers and those from whom support is sought. Personal meetings can, especially if an applicant is well prepared, furnish important information to potential contributors. Such contacts can likewise yield critical information to those seeking support—about which sorts of projects are likely to elicit positive responses, how plans might be modified to appear in a more favorable light, and so on. In the course of personal meetings, particularly where grant or other major proposals are being developed, there may result a sense of shared ownership between the two parties, even before a proposal has been given final form. Where a group or a consortium of institutions plans to approach a potential funding source, representatives of members of the group must be familiar with each other's advancement programs and needs and with the contribution that each will make to the projected venture. It is crucial to share this information with those from whom support is sought. Personal contacts are also often indispensable ingredients in the creation of the trust that is a precondition for gifts.

Conduct a Campus Visit. A prospect visit to campus can be a potent and convincing tool in the solicitation process. Nothing else can quite replace a first-hand view of the facilities, programs, students, and professional personnel of an institution seeking funds. Thorough preparation is mandatory. Faculty members and, especially, thoughtfully selected students who are well informed and enthusiastic can be the most effective ambassadors for a college or university during the visit. It is also true that exposing visitors to faculty members, staff, students, or others who are poorly informed about the institution or the concerns that a proposal addresses can be damaging.

Describe the Institution's Economic Impact. A growing number of colleges and universities have in recent years discovered the usefulness in fund raising of pertinent data about the economic impact of a campus on a local community, a county, a state, or even a wider area. Such data can often point to the existence of a reciprocal business or other relationship that a gift can make even more valuable by strengthening an institution. They can also confirm the existence, in the institution soliciting support, of a kind of business savvy that will appeal to its prospective contributors.

Put Together an Information Package. The final major step in preparing a strong case for gift support from new sources is the development and use of a well-designed institutional information package. The collection, formatting, and effective presentation of this information is a task that requires constant and highly skilled attention. At some point in the package the president or board chair of the institution needs to address candidly the prospect's questions as to reasons why support should be forthcoming. Direct and thoughtful answers indicate that an institution has given appropriate consideration to underlying issues. Professionalism is, increasingly, a necessary hallmark of these information packages, which are among a university's most important marketing devices. Officers to whom the development and presentation of such materials may be an unfamiliar task are well advised to study carefully the packages that successful competitors use—to engage in what management expert Tom Peters (1987) aptly calls "creative swiping" (p. 229)—as they complete their assignments.

Recognizing Donors

It is a given of fund raising that contributors, except in those rare instances in which anonymity is insisted on, desire appropriate recognition. Recognition itself can take any or several of a wide variety of forms. At one pole lies the conferral of an honorary degree, the naming of a building or a college or an endowment; at the other, a simple public announcement. Recipients of support should typically consider several measures.

Begin with a Thank-You. A visit or a letter to express appreciation is usually the beginning point for recognition. Most contributors want and deserve more. Follow-up reports about the longer-term impact of major gifts are easily arranged and much appreciated. They may also help pave the way for further contributions by cultivating goodwill as well as satisfaction that a grant made a difference and was well managed.

Involve Direct Beneficiaries of Gifts. As important as expressions of appreciation from major institutional officers may be, most givers also welcome written or oral testimony from those who benefited directly from a gift. A note from a faculty member who secured an urgently needed piece of equipment, from students who received scholarships made possible by current gifts or by contributions to endowment, or from those using a new facility is far more persuasive than a letter from a senior institutional officer. And such notes may also increase the donor's willingness to make a further contribution.

Send Special Publications. Publications may play a vital role in creating and strengthening linkages between potential givers and a campus. University and college advancement or public relations officers should maintain current prospect and donor files in their data banks so that they can send regular news and information pieces to these constituents. Receipt of such pieces can at once heighten a prospect's interest in an institution and hold out the attractive possibility of being featured in an appreciative story. Printed annual president's reports that list contributors for the year and even group them as to size of gift may serve the same purposes even more effectively. It is usually gratifying to be listed in the good company of well-known contributors and thereby to share in their prestige. The promise of a handsome, pictorially or graphically illustrated special publication celebrating an exceptional grant and depicting the giver and the recipients may be an even stronger inducement to grant support, as well as an effective public relations device. One caution to bear in mind, though, is that few contributors care to have the exact dollar amounts of their gifts reported. Unless special permission to do so is obtained, it is wise not to publish such information.

Final Words of Advice

A systematic effort to win new sources of external funding is well on the way to success if it follows the prescription offered here. It is important to emphasize a few key points by way of closing.

Don't Expect Miracles. Miracles, by definition, are rare, and they involve departures from the ordinary. In fund raising, this means that quick solutions and immediate results are uncommon. It is always theoretically possible that a major gift will suddenly materialize from some unexpected source and rescue a campus from disaster or meet some long-term need. But it is unlikely that this will happen. The cultivation of new giving constituents takes time, substantial investments of human and other resources, and patient, sustained effort.

Select People, Not Track Records, in Building Staff. Of course, records of success in fund raising are important indicators of the promise of future success. But other qualities may be even more important when the task is to select university or college advancement officers. Good oral and written communication skills, organizational talents, endurance, willingness to work long hours, and the ability to represent a cause effectively weigh heavily as qualifications. Sometimes the raw interest of a person already serving a campus in another capacity, combined with a willingness to complete training in fund raising, may prove to be a decisive consideration. The loyalty and zeal of alumni, even of retirees from a campus or from other professional careers, can also be major assets, as can a readiness on the part of such persons to accept challenging part-time or full-time positions on advancement staffs. One should not let a preoccupation with prior fund-raising experience divert consideration from candidates who possess less experience but who display desirable personal qualities in abundance. Select persons, not records.

Cultivation Is a Group Effort. New contributors are rarely won over through the efforts of presidents or board chairs working alone or even through the work of a tight inner circle of advancement professionals, however crucial these individuals might be in "closing" a transaction. The search for and nurture of new supporters must involve board members, volunteers, and faculty and professional staff members from across a campus, as well as top institutional officers. Everyone concerned can and must contribute to the effort—to collect information, to inventory and prioritize needs, to build the case, to present the needs, to cultivate and solicit the prospect who has been identified, to recognize the giver, and to do much else. Articulating the roles of the many participants in the effort and providing for the best use of their multiple talents are among the major tasks of leaders of the advancement effort.

Set Realistic Goals. Disappointment will surely come when efforts target unrealistically high dollar goals or aim for unrealistic numbers of new supporters. Cultivation of numerous prospects capable of making smaller contributions is less glamorous and more time-consuming and perhaps tedious than work with fewer potential big givers. It may, however, yield more sizable and enduring results. The fact is that a campus needs to generate support from a varied population capable of providing differing levels of support. There are relatively few individuals or entities capable of offering "the big gift." And it is always better to win one actual new contributor than the promise of ten.

Follow-Up Is Crucial. The work of the advancement team has only begun when a gift from a new supporter is finally in hand. The real task is to forge lasting linkages between the campus and the contributor. This task requires no less persistence and attention to detail than did the business of preparation, cultivation, and solicitation. It is through enduring relationships that colleges and universities stand the best chance of gaining the support that they need to perform their functions to best advantage.

To the certainties of death and taxes higher education administrators know that we must add another: Onrushing social change and the explosion of knowledge impose on colleges and universities constantly increasing demands for resources. The cultivation of new sources of external funding is not only one way of helping to meet these demands but it is also absolutely essential for institutional survival. It is therefore one of the most important forms of change that administrators must manage.

Reference

Peters, T. *Thriving on Chaos: A Handbook for a Management Revolution.* New York: Knopf, 1987.

Helmut Hofmann, formerly president of the Western Independent Colleges Fund and before that of Westminster College (Utah), is managing director of the European branch of City University, Bellevue, Washington.

*Often necessary to meet enrollment goals in a competitive age,
recruiting students from new sources requires a sound knowledge
of marketing, solid research, effective organization, and institutional
activities that will attract the desired populations.*

Targeting New Markets

Craig A. Green

In 1980, speaking before a group of college and university presidents in Des Moines, Iowa, Sandy Boyd, then president of the University of Iowa, defined "educational propensity" as "the act of recruiting students who were never born in the first place." Boyd's comment pointed to the sobering demographic reality confronting higher education as the 1980s opened. Many of the states in the Northeast and the Midwest faced declines of as much as 40 percent in the numbers of high school students graduating annually between 1975 and 1990. Even some of the more optimistic education planners foresaw the closure of between 5 and 8 percent of the weaker small private colleges by the mid 1990s and hard times for many larger institutions.

Colleges and universities are apparently emerging from the 1980s in better shape than anyone expected. An analysis of enrollment patterns over the last ten to twenty years shows clearly why they have done so well: They have redirected their product and service efforts toward an increasingly older student market. In the 1970s, most public and private institutions served students whom we term "traditional." Approximately 70 percent of total enrollment consisted of students who were eighteen to twenty-four years old, lived on campus, or studied full time. By 1990, the student population had increased 45 percent, from 8.6 million to some 12.5 million, but the proportion described as traditional had fallen by more than one-fifth, to 57 percent (U.S. Department of Commerce, 1989). The rest of the students are older, commute, or study part time. The arrival of these millions of new, nontraditional students is the chief reason for which the dire predictions of the 1970s, prophesying collapsing enrollments as the supply of traditional students shrank and impending cuts in federal funding for student financial aid eroded students' ability to pay for college, failed to come true. What is more, the "graying" of the campus so much in evidence today promises to persist indefinitely, as the national population continues to age.

The student mix that is now common has brought a significant change in the way that colleges and universities do business. Academic scheduling, admissions policies and practices, curricula and modes of teaching, and the entire range of student services have had to adjust. It is also true that many of the institutions that have experienced shifts in the composition and character of their student population did not anticipate, plan for, or intentionally organize for the changes that their aging and often more demanding students have forced. Instead, many campuses only belatedly discovered that their clientele had changed and turned to some retromarketing and measures to serve the academic and nonacademic needs of their new student bodies. Numbers of institutions, particularly private colleges, still cling to the belief that sometime in the future the good old days will return, and classrooms will again echo with the chatter and laughter of legions of traditional students with their familiar needs.

In order for higher education to succeed in the 1990s and the following decades, it must substantially improve its ability to anticipate the future—and then to deal with the future.

Introduction to Marketing Principles for Higher Education

Over the last forty years, there have occurred many changes in the admissions function within higher education. Admissions personnel have evolved from paper pushers to gatekeepers and screeners, then to advertisers and wranglers, then to marketers, and, finally, to enrollment managers. As both public and private colleges and universities have become more and more enrollment driven, the role of enrollment management professionals as key participants in the institutional planning process has gained in importance. With the acceptance of enrollment management as an institutional necessity, rather than a slogan, enrollment marketing will become a major element of the academic scene.

Marketing Defined. The proper beginning point for a discussion of educational marketing is a definition of the term. Philip Kotler (1975), a pioneer in the field, wrote:

> Marketing is the analysis, planning, implementation, and control of carefully formulated programs designed to bring about voluntary exchanges of values with target markets for the purpose of achieving organizational objectives. It relies heavily on designing the organization's offering in terms of target markets' needs and desires, and on using effective pricing,

communication, and distribution to inform, motivate, and service the markets (p. 5).

In a speech, Robert Peck (1982), formerly vice president for campus services of the Council of Independent Colleges, defined marketing more succinctly, as "the systematic cultivation of exchanges between the college or university and its various publics which (1) promote the mission of the institution and (2) meet the needs of the publics."

Three Marketing Approaches. Before any institution can set out to market itself to its various publics, whether students, potential students, donors, alumni, community leaders, or others, it must first decide what its product is or is going to be. In the 1970s, Americans faced a basic choice between the two biggest fast-food chains, McDonald's and Burger King. In the McDonald's operation, all hamburgers were the same. All were served with the same condiments and to the accompaniment of the slogan, "We do it all for you." Burger King, in contrast, attempted to provide flexibility in both product and ambience by offering to add or delete options and by persuading customers that "special orders don't upset us." Similarly, educational institutions must decide what kinds of hamburgers they are going to offer to students and how.

Target marketing depends on the act of segmenting the market or, in other words, on identifying the various classes of actual and potential consumers and their distinctive needs and desires. Having segmented the market, the college or university must choose from among three broad marketing strategies outlined in Kotler and Fox's (1985) *Strategic Marketing for Educational Institutions*. The choices are as follows:

1. Undifferentiated, or mass, marketing—An institution using this approach makes a single offer to the entire market, seeking thereby to attract as many students as possible.

2. Differentiated marketing—This option involves identifying several different market segments (that is, target populations with determinate needs) and developing separate offers to serve the desired segments in a fashion that will maximize enrollment.

3. Concentrated marketing—Pursuing this choice, an institution decides to address only a single market segment and to develop an ideal offer and a marketing plan to attract as many students from that segment as may be desired.

One or another of these three broad marketing strategies will already be in place at every college and university, whether by conscious design or by happenstance. The approach in operation is ordinarily a product of the mission or founding intent of the institution, of tradition, or, much less often, of some recent decision to redirect the institution. A major change of strategy is not often an option, and it probably should not be, since consistency of mission is a basic tenet of American higher education.

Two New Market Options. The potential for identifying and serving the needs of new target markets exists for any college or university that seeks to maintain or enhance its enrollment. Regardless of the level of sophistication of its marketing efforts or its past marketing record, there are available only two real options for use in targeting new markets. These are offering an old product to a new market or offering a new product to a new market. Institutions of higher education most often pursue the former option because it is usually easier and much less costly to market programs currently in existence when it is to develop and offer new programs with uncertain prospects for success. No matter which option is elected, the development of a marketing plan will involve the same elements. Discussion of these elements follows.

Measurement Against Mission. At the outset of consideration of a new marketing approach, either the proposed program or the market to be solicited or both must be measured against the institution's mission. Planners must ask whether or not the program or the potential market fits the institutional mission. If the answer is no, then it will be essential to inquire whether the change that will result will be for the better or for the worse.

Research. Research is the most important component of a marketing effort. Basic research need not be costly, but it must be conducted with professional expertise, and it will take time to complete. Frequently, campuses contain on their faculties professors who are knowledgeable about marketing and marketing research and who can supervise staff research activities. Where this is not the case, it may be necessary to engage the services of an expert consultant. The research will need to include, at a minimum, initial focus groups to be surveyed, well-conceived survey instruments, an assessment of the external (usually demographic) environment, and a survey of relevant aspects of the competition. It is particularly important that the most obvious competitor programs and institutions be studied in the course of the research. Decisions about projected marketing efforts will be made largely on the basis of reigning perceptions about the degree of saturation or of unsatisfied demand that is present. The competition survey needs to determine, in addition, the answers to two fundamental questions: First, what is the competition doing and how well? Second, how well do competitors communicate about their products to the market? Of the many publications available about market research for enrollment management, readers may find it especially helpful to consult Ingersoll's (1988) *The Enrollment Problem.*

Planning. Research will yield general directions for the marketing approach, communications efforts, publications needed, and timing. All of these factors need to be budgeted and scheduled. The common assumption is that planning for a marketing initiative will not require much time. As a result, too little time is typically allotted for planning. During the course of planning, it will be vital to develop a calendar for the new effort. It will also be crucial to bear in mind that the new program will probably not supplant any existing administrative or marketing activity, for a new thrust is almost always launched as an addition to normal marketing efforts.

Execution. If the research and planning activities have been properly completed, the execution of the plan can go forward with minimal difficulty. Campus officers must remember, however, that they must provide sufficient resources and staff personnel to carry the effort to success. It is also essential to ensure that the staff receives proper training and the direction needed to encourage effective performance.

Evaluation. Evaluation should contain a continuous (formative) component and a final (summative) component. It should address both the enrollment results of the new initiative and its financial outcomes in terms of return on investment and of dollar results measured against expectations. The evaluation process should contain a component of market research, too. This research will address the target audience and key decision makers, the students who have newly enrolled as a result of the plan, the staff and faculty members most affected by changes issuing from the plan, and, where appropriate, relevant external publics. Ordinarily, these external publics will include such groups as business or corporate leaders, clergy, and others who contributed advice and ideas that informed the program.

The final evaluation should accomplish two additional things. It should establish a process for assessing the new market effort continuously in the future. And it should ascertain how closely final outcomes met institutional expectations. In dealing with this last question, administrators should bear in mind that no new program or marketing venture ever exactly meets the intended objectives and that the assessment process must consider how much deviance from the original goals and how much adjustment of goals are tolerable.

An Example of Success in Targeting New Markets

The experience of Westminster College of Salt Lake City since 1980 shows how an institution can increase enrollment by targeting new markets. A great many colleges and universities think of themselves as unique and advertise their distinctiveness as a means of attracting students, even though they share many characteristics in common with numerous other campuses. Westminster's situation is, however, unusual in several respects. In the Midwest and Northeast, there are hundreds of small, private institutions that claim a liberal arts orientation. In Utah there is only one such institution—Westminster. Westminster is located just one mile from a major state university, the University of Utah, and just forty miles from the largest private university in the world, Brigham Young. Westminster operates in a state usually thought of as rural because so much of it is sparsely inhabited. But Utah, when the proportion of its population living in areas defined by the federal census as urban is taken into account, turns out to be the most urban of all the states. More than 92 percent of its population lives within a seventy-mile strip city running from Ogden in the north through Salt Lake City to Provo in the south. The people of the Beehive State, consequently, display an overwhelmingly high level of economic, consumer, and even educational sophistication.

Crisis. In the late 1970s, Westminster was in serious financial difficulty, primarily as a result of ineffective leadership. On several occasions and as late as 1982, at the direction of the governing board the college's administration was preparing plans for the legal protection of officers and institutional assets in the event of closure. Enrollment had been declining for a decade, to a low of 1,080 in 1981. The college had always been a small school with few funds available for growth or even operations. It had never, since its founding in 1875, seen really prosperous years.

Revitalization. Creative leadership and a redirection of marketing efforts to recruit both new students and new financial support have led the way in achieving unprecedented success for Westminster since 1982. The support of the metropolitan community, which has responded enthusiastically to the college's progress, has also contributed significantly to its improving circumstances. By the fall of 1989, enrollment had grown beyond 2,000. All of the institution's debts, including a cumulative operating deficit that had haunted it for fifty years, had been paid. Major construction projects are now disrupting the life of the campus. A functional and flexible strategic plan directs budgets and annual operations, as it has since Westminster's revival began.

Students continue now, as always, to generate most of Westminster's income. During the fiscal year 1988–89, students were the source of 80 percent of operating revenues. The crucial importance of income derived from students has assigned top priority to enrollment efforts.

Role of New Markets. Success in tapping new markets has been central to Westminster's revival. In particular, the college has targeted four key populations. These are nontraditional (especially transfer) students; students pursuing the master of business administration (MBA) degree (a new program); nursing students, particularly registered nurses seeking to complete the baccalaureate degree; and current students of every description, for whom the object is improved retention. In seeking to reach these market segments, Westminster has systematically and continuously employed all of the marketing activities described earlier. While the degree of success in using these activities has varied from time to time, the college has nevertheless been able to expand its enrollment consistently.

Nontraditional and transfer students now comprise more than 60 percent of Westminster's enrollment. No longer willing to allow a traditional semester calendar to dictate marketing efforts, the college has made it possible for students to enter at the beginning of any of five terms. Currently, only about 65 percent of new students enter during the fall term. We have actively developed articulation agreements with several area community and technical colleges, and we have responded positively to an invitation to join with the four-year public universities in defining standards for evaluating students' general education work and for easing the transfer of credits between participating institutions.

Westminster's MBA program originated in 1981. It aimed to provide high-quality instruction in flexibly scheduled classes and to increase enrollment. At present, 340 students are pursuing the degree, up from ten when the program began. The program is widely regarded as one of the best such regional degree courses for working adults.

Westminster undertook nursing education in the 1960s by assimilating a local hospital's diploma school and converting it to a baccalaureate school. When the 1980s opened, poor enrollment and the high costs associated with maintaining a program enjoying National League for Nursing accreditation pushed the college to the brink of a decision to close the school of nursing. New leadership and a calculated turn of direction to recruit heavily among registered nurses desiring to complete baccalaureate degrees and among local residents have resulted in burgeoning enrollments. The school of nursing is now filled to capacity and is turning away students.

Currently enrolled students comprise Westminster's other major new target market. Like too many other institutions, the college had long suffered from poor retention of students. Even when adequate numbers came for the first term of the year, high attrition created problems during succeeding terms. In the 1980s the administration and the faculty—who are the crucial group for bettering retention—joined in a major retention effort. As a result, retention has improved by 25 percent in the last five years.

Westminster, despite its striking growth, firmly intends to remain a small college. Although expanding enrollment has brought new problems—for the first time there are student complaints about closed classes, full parking lots, and long lines in the cafeteria and the coffee shop—the campus has retained its essential character. Westminster has maintained a seventeen-to-one student-faculty ratio and its ability to offer personalized education. It continues its program of intensive academic advising provided by faculty and staff professionals.

Westminster's Marketing Efforts

Marketing at Westminster involves a wide spectrum of activities. Other institutions that wish to target new markets or to serve their existing markets better might find some or all of these to be useful. The most important are described here.

Organization for Marketing. Functional assignments have replaced geographic and territorial assignments for admissions personnel at Westminster. Some people specialize in serving graduate students; some, transfers; others, readmits; and still others, freshmen. Faculty members do not evaluate the records of transfer applicants. Instead, the admissions professional who works with transfer students does. The use of functional assignments allows the development of skilled specialists who can provide superior marketing efforts for target groups and superior service to them. It is also desirable to assign specific admissions activities, such as communication, publications, advertising, church relations, special projects, campus visitations, faculty outreach, and the like, to individual staff members.

Once organized, the admissions office should operate on an eighteen-month calendar of activities that is updated annually. The calendar facilitates goal setting, effective deployment of resources, and wise scheduling of operations. It also encourages thoughtful planning for and completion of evaluation of outcomes.

The creation of an enrollment management task force has been most important. This group brings together admissions, financial aid, and student service professionals with other key administrators and selected faculty members. It works with enrollment management professional staff members to plan toward improving the quality of incoming students and enhancing student retention. The task force can be a valuable conduit through which to disseminate information to and solicit ideas and support from the faculty.

Admissions staff training and professional development are vital. Provision of out-of-office reading time on a regular basis is a useful development strategy. Of more immediate importance is the need to ensure that staff members are always current on the capabilities and uses of campus computing services as providers of needed information. Ongoing training in computer use and regular receipt of computer-generated information and reports are essential for increasing the productivity of admissions staff members.

Westminster uses various advisory boards and councils, as well as its board of trustees, to assist in marketing. These bodies regularly receive reports and enjoy opportunities to frame and forward ideas and otherwise provide help. Creation of a standing committee of an institution's governing board to oversee enrollment issues is an important step. Such a committee should contain at least some members who are professionally employed in not-for-profit organizations.

A last organizational task is to ensure that effort is not duplicated unintentionally. If several campus units are responsible for recruiting or retaining students, valuable resources may be wasted. Efficiency matters.

Research and Consultants. Research and the advice of professional consultants are needed for an effective marketing program. At Westminster, we have learned that major research for enrollment management purposes must be repeated not less often than once every four years. Student bodies and student needs change greatly over a four-year period. Old research findings quickly become obsolete. New research will reveal in which ways communications and admissions programs need to be adjusted. The adjustments are apt to be considerable insofar as a campus depends on traditional students. Any research four or more years old should be destroyed. If it is retained, someone will read it and assume that it is worth something. Its age ensures that it is not.

There is a great deal of free research data available to colleges and universities, and most campuses harbor faculty members with expertise in marketing. Both should be used. Local advertising agencies, radio and television stations, and even other institutions of higher education will often share their research findings free of charge. Knowledgeable faculty members can frequently deal with problems and short-term issues more quickly and less expensively than can outside consultants. Making use of local faculty members can also nourish good relations between enrollment and marketing officers and the faculty.

Researchers must recognize that students are the best source of information on some issues. This is true, for example, when there are questions about the academic calendar or class schedules. Students, however, cannot solve problems. That is the job of administrators and faculty members.

External consultants will typically be helpful about once very six years and perhaps more often on campuses that are still developing their enrollment management programs. Consultants can often design and conduct needed research, audit admissions programs, and assist in shaping marketing efforts. There are several good firms in the business at present. None is inexpensive, but there is risk of much greater expense, in terms of lost income because students did not enroll, if consultants are not used.

Finally, it is a good idea to share research findings through as many campus channels as possible. Honest and open sharing builds trust. It frequently prompts different and useful interpretations of the data and other helpful responses. The enrollment management task force can be a particularly valuable vehicle for sharing findings and soliciting responses.

Scholarships and Financial Aid. Pricing is one of the most important marketing tools. The establishment of a tuition rate is a decision that helps determine an institution's competitive position. Scholarships and financial aid programs connect to pricing by affecting the actual cost to students and in some cases by siphoning off new institutional funds secured through tuition increases for payment to aid and scholarship recipients. We have learned that we must reassess our financial aid operation no less often than every two years. Proper use of institutional funds holds high priority, for, like most campuses, we have limited resources for financial aid.

At Westminster, aid and scholarship efforts are related. We have moved away from a "first-come, first-served, high-priority-for-highest-need" approach. Instead, we use aid dollars to shape the character of our student population in desired ways. The introduction of no-need, merit-based scholarships for both entering freshmen and transfer students has been a major instrument in this effort. The college offers academic scholarships automatically with admission to applicants who meet the stated criteria. The number of such awards is limited only by the number of qualified applicants. Applicants need submit no paperwork beyond what is required for admission—a completed application form, transcripts, references, test scores. The new scholarships have led in attracting academically more talented students and in improving the college's image. Average American College Testing program scores of entering freshmen have risen from 19 to about 22 over a period of about five years, and one-fourth of entering freshmen stand in the upper quintile of their classes, with scores of 25 or better.

A related concern is to track the tuition reimbursement policies of major area employers. Knowledge in this area will assist greatly in identifying promising sources of prospective students. It will also enable a campus to serve better its students who are fully employed. Someone on the admissions staff should be responsible for gathering the relevant data.

Presentation of the Institution. Westminster presents itself as a student-oriented college that offers personalized, high-quality instruction aimed at preparing graduates for careers and productive lives while grounding them in the liberal arts. In seeking to meet the needs of students, we offer flexible payment plans. The days of "pay when you register at the beginning of the term" are gone. We have also eliminated virtually all "nuisance fees." These include charges designed chiefly to influence the behavior of traditional students. They also include admissions application, graduation, add or drop, parking, student identification, and some late fees. Tuition now makes up for income lost when these charges were abandoned.

For many years, Westminster offered classes at several off-campus sites to make study more convenient to employed students. It turned out that the concept was more attractive to the college than to students, who preferred to come to the campus even if it was for only one evening class meeting weekly. Other institutions might wish to examine the question of off-campus sites with care. Even if they prove to be attractive to students, they might not add to enrollment. Because our students prefer to come to the campus, the appearance of the campus is even more important than it would otherwise be. Knowing this, Westminster maintains its buildings and grounds in excellent condition.

Communications, publication, fieldwork by admissions representatives, and other forms of outreach are among the chief means of presenting a college or university. Westminster's viewbook and other publications have all been designed to serve their intended functions and to meet the needs of target audiences. Their appearance, organization, and contents all reflect their purposes and draw on market research. We add to these efforts press releases featuring college-related human interest stories, because local newspapers prefer such stories to statistical reports about enrollment. The alumni magazine regularly reports admissions news. Personal recruiting efforts by our deans of business and nursing have been important sources of students, too. Such activity can be effective on many campuses.

Test marketing is an extension of the other ways in which an institution presents itself. Each year, using research data, the enrollment management staff must designate, develop, and review primary, secondary, tertiary, and test market segments. All of these must be evaluated regularly.

Faculty. The faculty is at the center of any successful marketing effort. There is no substitute in marketing for excellent teaching. Superb teaching continues to be a main source of student satisfaction, and satisfied customers are still, as always, the best recruiters for any campus. Faculty members can be helpful outside of the classroom, too. Telephone responses to inquiries about programs can make a difference. Intrusive, concerned advising of students can make a difference. Program development can make a difference. Westminster's success in attracting able students had to be matched with the development of a new honors program to serve them. The program, in turn, became a marketing tool. Whatever faculty members do that is helpful needs to be valued and publicly recognized.

Conclusion

The art of targeting new markets is not particularly difficult, if the proper methods are employed. It may be a bit riskier than some campuses would wish, but it is a necessary element in the enrollment management efforts of most colleges and universities in this age of competition.

References

Ingersoll, R. *The Enrollment Problem.* New York: American Council on Education/ Macmillan, 1988.

Kotler, P. *Marketing for Nonprofit Organizations.* Englewood Cliffs, N.J.: Prentice-Hall, 1975.

Kotler, P., and Fox, K.F.A. *Strategic Marketing for Higher Education.* Englewood Cliffs, N.J.: Prentice-Hall, 1985.

Peck, R. "Strategic Planning for Small Private Colleges." Keynote address at the Council of Independent Colleges Conference on Strategic Planning, Chicago, October 1982.

U.S. Department of Commerce. *Statistical Abstract of the United States, 1989.* (109th ed.) Washington, D.C.: U.S. Government Printing Office, 1989.

Craig A. Green is vice-president for enrollment management at Westminster College, Salt Lake City, Utah.

Lynchburg College's Program for Institutional Change offers one model for the adaptations that higher education must make in order to reply to the fact that by the year 2020 one of every three Americans will be a member of a minority group.

The Demographic Imperative: Changing to Serve America's Expanding Minority Population

George N. Rainsford

According to various authoritative estimates, by somewhere between the years 2000 and 2020 one out of every three Americans will not be white. Already, every one of the nation's twenty-five largest school districts serves a minority majority.

This demographic shift poses both a challenge and an opportunity to higher education. The introduction to the American Council on Higher Education's handbook, *Minorities on Campus* (Green, 1989), puts the issue directly: Although the nation's minority population, taken as a whole, is growing, minority enrollment in higher education is falling. Between 1975 and 1985, the share of blacks of college age who entered colleges and universities fell from 48 to 44 percent, that of Hispanics from 51 to 47 percent, while in 1985 only 17 percent of Native American youths enrolled. Minority students who undertook postsecondary studies were also less likely than whites to earn a degree.

Families, high schools, and communities can all do things to help turn the situation around. But leadership must come from our colleges and universities, and they in turn must change if they are to become and are to be perceived to have become more hospitable institutions to minority students, faculty, and staff. This chapter considers how colleges and universities can best serve minority populations and offers the experience of Lynchburg College, a private, church-related, coeducational, residential institution in Virginia, as one model for change.

NEW DIRECTIONS FOR HIGHER EDUCATION, no. 71, Fall 1990 ©Jossey-Bass Inc., Publishers

Efforts to Provide Equity in Access in the 1960s and 1970s

With the flowering of the civil rights movement in the 1960s, America discovered its conscience with regard to its minority population. The relatively new medium of television brought into the nation's living rooms a vivid and disturbing portrayal of prejudice and discrimination. A sense of guilt about past and present wrongs, now publicly admitted, joined with a swelling concern about social justice that sought to provide equity for black Americans and members of other minority groups. One result was a highly publicized effort to mainstream minority persons into the nation's social, business, and educational institutions through the imposition of quotas or goals for minority recruitment.

But these minority Americans did not become a part of the main fabric of our colleges and universities. Rather, they were added to or grafted on to these institutions of higher learning as extras. Educational institutions typically did not change their missions to include a commitment to minority persons. By and large, colleges and universities failed to provide the support services that the new students needed. Colleges and universities took credit for enrolling minority students but did not commit themselves to seeing that they graduated. What mattered in the context of meeting civil rights objectives were the numbers enrolled for the first time, rather than successful accomplishments leading to graduation. Thus, while the front door was open, so was the back door.

It is clear that this approach failed, both in the short term and the long term. Minority students were enrolled in institutions that were unprepared to provide either the remedial academic preparation required to ready them for collegiate studies or the academic and nonacademic support necessary to help them survive and succeed in an alien cultural environment. In many cases, colleges and universities did not even trouble themselves to find out what support systems were either necessary or desirable.

Resting on an inadequate understanding of the extent and depth of commitment required to serve minority students adequately, efforts of the 1960s and 1970s to achieve educational equity for these students failed to meet their objective. This experience taught us that unless institutions of higher education changed their missions so as to make enrollment of minority students and provision to those students of services required to make graduation a likely outcome a central, rather than a peripheral, concern, efforts to recruit and educate such students would prove to be largely fruitless.

Higher Education as Economic Resource Development in the 1980s and 1990s

If a concern for social justice fueled minority recruitment efforts in the 1960s and 1970s, a new economic concern did so in the 1980s. In a competitive global economy, the young—the nation's future work force—have increasingly come to be seen as a crucial economic resource. Their education has come to figure importantly in discussions of ways to maintain an efficient and competitive economy. If a significant portion of our new national population is to consist of minority groups, then we need to educate them, to develop that resource, for the nation's economic advantage as well as for theirs. If our institutions of higher education can learn to serve the rapidly growing numbers of minority persons, these people will be an enormous asset. If our colleges and universities do not learn to do so, these people will be an enormous liability, in terms both of the direct costs to society of increased unemployment, crime, needs for welfare programs, and demand for public health care and of the indirect cost represented by reduced competitiveness in the international economic arena.

The new minority populations will also be an important resource for our colleges and universities. As increasing numbers of their members rise toward and into middle-class, middle-income status and acquire the desire and the preparation to pursue a college education, they will become a crucial source of students.

The success of the educational job that we do for our new minority population will have both internal and international implications. Our capacity to respond constructively to the disastrous condition of the nation's mainly minority urban schools will properly be a test of our capacity to deal with the entire range of school problems across the country. Moreover, the same capacity, or lack of it, will be seen as the indicator of our intentions with regard to the mainly nonwhite Third World, which will loom increasingly large on the international scene.

We have been called on as a nation to "solve" our public school problems. At the core of these problems is our urban, poor, minority population, and this circumstance will only become more pronounced. The issue for our colleges and universities is to define their role in providing solutions to this national problem. We can begin by doing a better job in higher education, by devising a strategy and posing for ourselves a higher expectation for success in dealing with our own minority populations. If our colleges and universities do not learn to do so, then the resulting mass of undereducated minority persons may become an enormous liability.

Starting the Process of Change

The most important point to understand is that change is required; business as usual will not get the job done.

Start with the Institutional Mission. The mission of our colleges and universities must be expanded to include a commitment to recruit minority students, faculty, and staff. The commitment must be broad enough and realistic enough to ensure the financial and support services needed to implement the new mission. Serving a new minority population must not be something that our institutions do in addition to their regular work. It must be understood to be part of their regular work.

Provide Leadership Commitment. Change must start at the top, with the full support of the institution's governing board and of the president. The commitment will not be perceived as real if the board and the president merely tell others what to do and are not doing so themselves.

Develop a Plan with Measurable and Assessable Goals. Unplanned change or change without specified goals may miss the mark. It may also fail to establish the objectives that the community as a whole can agree to and accept.

Seek Broad Participation from the Campus Community. Broad ownership and responsibility will flow from broad participation. Change is seldom successful when it is only imposed from the top. Wide involvement will also elicit new ideas and new visions of what is needed and what will work.

Assign Responsibility to Individuals. Communities and committees can only accept general responsibility for policy formulation or oversight. The tasks that make a plan work must be assigned to individuals who possess the authority and responsibility to carry them out.

Schedule a Timetable. Difficult tasks often need deadlines to ensure that they get done. Meeting deadlines, in turn, develops a sense of accomplishment and therefore of forward movement and progress.

Assess and Build on Results. Mechanisms with which to evaluate progress toward goals should be built into the efforts to change. When there is success, planners should build on it in setting the next round of goals. When there is not, reexamining goals to determine whether or not they are realistic and whether or not the efforts to achieve them were well directed and sufficient is necessary.

Institutionalize the Change Process. Incorporating the process of generating and sustaining change into the fabric of the institution allows continued success to occur even through and beyond changes in leadership. This is the hardest part of all—to make the program a part of the core activities and commitments of a college or university, rather than a mere add-on or an afterthought.

Be Prepared for Setbacks as Well as Advances. Change does not usually take place through a steady linear progression of orderly advances or through giant steps forward. It usually comes about as a result of the persistent and consistent application of pressure at the margins. The gains sometimes seem small. But as they accumulate, their impact is great. Thus, it is all right to be in a hurry. It is also all right to make mistakes, as long as learning results.

Use Fund Raising as Evidence of Commitment and Success. Good intentions are rarely an adequate foundation on which to build change. People must invest in change if it is to become a reality. Nothing will more quickly convince faculty and other members of an academic community that an idea is a good one than the ability of the institution to raise money in support of it.

A Model. In 1986, Lynchburg College's president urged the Lynchburg academic community to take the lead in recognizing that soon one out of every three Americans would not be white and that Lynchburg, as an essentially white, Southern, church-related, residential institution, held an obligation to make itself more hospitable to minority students. As a result, Lynchburg initiated the Program for Institutional Change. It recruited a leading black educator to membership on the board of trustees. It hired a young and successful black graduate as assistant to the president, with responsibility as the principal officer in the Program for Institutional Change. It attracted a major grant from the Jessie B. duPont Foundation to support the program. It formed an advisory committee composed of representatives of all elements of the college. It set a five-year goal of achieving an enrollment of 9 to 10 percent minority students. Realism resulted in setting a less precise goal for the hiring of minority faculty and staff personnel. Now the Lynchburg administration delivers to the granting foundation and the college community regular and periodic reports on the progress of the program. The admissions staff has added minority persons to make certain that the minority student recruitment effort is ongoing and energetic. The student life area has likewise added minority staff personnel to provide role models and support systems. The college's first full-time black regular faculty member has joined the Department of History.

Recruiting Students

As noted earlier, a fruitful minority student recruitment program must grow out of the institutional mission. The mission should include and, if necessary, should be modified to incorporate a commitment to valuing diversity within the institution. A successful recruitment effort will also involve several measures that apply specifically to the admissions plan.

Use Financial Aid. If an institution is serious in its intent to educate young minority women and men, it will not merely increase financial aid funding, thereby raising the bidding for a static pool of minority students, but it will also work hard to employ aid resources so as to enlarge the pool of minority high school students for whom college is a realistic option. Financial aid is both a help and a hindrance in minority student recruitment. Many minority families are not familiar with the aid system and find it threatening, particularly when they are asked to reveal fiscal data about which they may be embarrassed. There is thus a real need for sympathetic, comprehensive budget counseling for high school students and their parents, showing how college is affordable and how to make financial ends meet while in college.

Increase the Pool. There are many ways to enlarge the applicant pool.

Working with appropriate secondary schools for early identification of able minority students is essential. Establishing transition programs for these students—working with families, counselors, and teachers to make sure that the students complete the right courses and understand that college attendance is a possibility—is helpful. Nearby community colleges may prove to be sources of another important population: transfer students. It is fruitful to develop close contacts with community colleges, to track appropriate students, and, if necessary, to provide financial aid and scholarship programs directed specifically toward transfers.

Bet on Leadership. In identifying minority students with potential for college success, an institution must be willing to bet on leadership, even if it is not expressed academically. Leadership in other areas often becomes the basis for building self-confidence that, in turn, nourishes academic success. As long as all graduates meet the same exit requirements, it is not lowering standards to take a risk by admitting some students who appear to be weak academically but strong as leaders.

Provide Orientation Programs. Summer transition programs and other orientation efforts on the college or university campus help introduce high school students to understand life and work, affording them familiarity with and confidence in their ability to work in the academic environment. It is particularly important in a precollege orientation plan to incorporate work with campus housing for students who are not used to campus residential life.

Offer Retention Programs. Early testing and provision of feedback on the results can be used to develop self-confidence and survival habits in students. Undergraduate success, however, is less involved with simply getting in than it is with gaining confidence that one can succeed after having begun. Like other students, minority students come with different needs. Use of peer counselors and of successful role models drawn from alumni and the local minority community helps to meet these needs. This is particularly important if there is not a critical mass of minority faculty and staff members available to counsel and serve as role models.

A Model. Lynchburg College has developed successful programs for recruiting and retaining minority students. Working particularly with nearby Virginia high schools, Lynchburg has developed financial aid programs for both regularly college-bound students and less academically focused but high-potential students who qualify for leadership grants. High school early-identification measures and college summer orientation events have been valuable. Leading black alumni from the region and instructors from high schools and the local community college have acted as adult role models while the college works to develop a critical mass of its own minority faculty and staff. Many of the students transferring from the community college with Lynchburg College scholarships have been minority students. Once admitted, minority students receive close monitoring and support from the director of the Program for Institutional Change and her staff. Their retention has therefore been better than average, as have their grade point averages. Regular and ongoing financial counseling with students and parents has been an added help.

Recruiting Faculty and Staff

The recruitment of minority faculty and staff personnel, as of students, begins with the strategies treated in the section on starting the process of change. The first step is to make it clear that such recruitment is part of the institution's mission and will be supported with resources and organized efforts.

Use the Personnel Office. The personnel office should be recognized and regularly used as a key resource in recruitment. It can help standardize searches to include minority searches, train search teams to make use of minority networks, and advertise aggressively. The institution must also make it clear to program supervisors and department chairs that adding minority personnel, as an important objective, will be rewarded. There must be a willingness, as well, to meet the market price for such persons.

Stay in Touch with Graduate Schools and with Successful Alumni. These can be important "inside" sources of names. They should be exploited.

Network. There are numerous possibilities for cooperating with other institutions. These include arrangements for faculty exchanges with black or other minority institutions, provision of fellowships for visiting minority professors, or creation of joint appointments with nearby four-year and two-year institutions or possibly even high schools.

Maintain a Single Standard. Minority faculty and staff members must be held to the same performance standards as others to prevent the growth of a perception that an institution harbors both first- and second-class professionals. A common standard unites and strengthens; multiple standards divide and weaken.

Seek Minority Individuals to Serve Across the Institution. Minority faculty and staff members should be recruited across the entire institution. Such recruitment should start at the top, at the president's office, and proceed next to the personnel office. Beginnings in these key areas will make it easier to extend the effort to other realms, while recruitment across the campus will prevent the channeling or maneuvering of minority persons merely into positions or career paths traditionally reserved for them.

A Model. After hiring a black graduate as assistant to the president, Lynchburg College added black staff members in the personnel, housing, admissions, financial aid, student life, and library areas. A black community college professor served as an adjunct faculty member in speech and a doctorally prepared black person joined the history department. Lynchburg is currently undertaking a sister relationship with a private, historically black Virginia university. Searches for faculty and staff members now require aggressive affirmative action measures.

Transforming the Campus Community

While an institution may contain particular programs or vehicles for change, success in transforming a whole campus cannot occur unless the academic community has accepted the necessity of change and has come to support the efforts to change with respect to both people and educational offerings. Pervasive institutional change requires broad-ranging efforts and acceptance.

Provide Leadership from the Top. There must be continued and visible leadership from the governing board and the president to keep the program on course and directed toward the entire institution. Continued advocacy from the top for budget support is one good gauge of leadership.

Overcome the Myths and Confront the Reality. Campuses seeking to diversify ethnically and racially must confront two dominant myths. The first is that there is no racism on campus. Change agents must first confront the myth and then accept and deal with the reality that there is racism on most campuses, although this racism is usually sublimated and less explicit than that on the assembly line. The second myth is that all minority young people are poor, disadvantaged, and unprepared for higher education. In reality, while this description applies to numbers of both minority and majority young persons, there is a growing, educated, affluent, and successful minority middle class whose children are bound for college.

Encourage Campus Recognition and Acceptance of Minority Cultures. The addition of minority students, faculty, and staff will inject an element of diversity into an institution. But institutional change will be minimal unless the campus majority population learns to embrace the obligation and the opportunity to understand and appreciate minority cultures and the contributions that they can make.

Pay Attention to Symbols. Much of what colleges do unconsciously reflects the majority culture of our society. If an institution seeks to make a place for minority persons, attention to symbols is important. Display in the president's, dean's, and admissions offices of copies of *Ebony*, as well as of *Time*, *Newsweek*, and *National Geographic*, makes a statement. So does the presence in the college store of ethnically oriented merchandise.

Recognize the Risks. Institutional change is value-laden. A campus must recognize that a program to increase racial or ethnic diversity will alienate some old constituents and attract some new ones. But it is vital to advance change—to be on the side of the future, rather than merely that of the past.

Work with Local High Schools. Local high schools, some of them under a state mandate to act, are finding it particularly hard to recruit minority faculty members. Colleges and local school systems can work together in identifying and recruiting minority instructors. They can also work together in ventures to increase the number of minority persons qualified to teach.

Develop an Appropriate Grievance Procedure. Diversifying a campus racially requires the recruitment of minority students, faculty members, and staff persons, *and* a change of attitude toward racism. Besides adopting and implementing a mission statement that values diversity, a college or university needs to develop a grievance procedure that provides a well-understood mechanism to employ when incidents of racism occur.

A Model. Lynchburg College's Program for Institutional Change began with a strong statement about the desirability of diversity and with the recruitment of minority persons to the governing board and the president's staff. Many other measures followed. The college maintains a year-round effort to highlight black culture. It sponsors a monthlong series of black history programs, which have attracted national speakers and programs, that involves both the campus and the community. Lynchburg students have formed a new gospel choir. They have formed a chapter of a national black service organization, Alpha Kappa Alpha Sorority, and they are planning the organization of a chapter of a like fraternity. The college president's reception area displays copies of *Equal Opportunity*. Each fall, minority high school seniors recommended by their guidance counselors receive invitations to a three-day program that gives them an opportunity to visit the college, attend classes, and experience campus life. The same program is repeated for juniors in the spring. The college has also worked with the local public school system to provide special scholarships for minority teacher assistants who wish to become fully certified teachers and remain in the area. The awards support study in both undergraduate and graduate education programs. Finally, there is a widely shared and accurate sense that there is less racism on the Lynchburg campus now than there was five years ago.

Conclusion

The demographic facts about the growth of the nation's minority population are clear. The country's colleges and universities must radically change their structures, values, hiring practices, and treatment of students if they are to meet the demographic shift and attract more minority students, faculty members, and staff personnel. Considerations of social equity, national economic efficiency, and—as minority population growth continues while the relative supply of white students falls—institutional survival argue strongly for change. This change will require massive new resources only if colleges and universities attempt to add the achievement of racial or cultural diversity to everything else that they do, rather than making it part of their core mission and activity.

There is a growing body of relevant literature that can easily be identified in most academic libraries through an Educational Resources Information Center (ERIC) search. Perhaps the best single volume about enhancing campus racial and cultural diversity is *Minorities on Campus* (Green, 1989), referred to earlier. Also useful are volumes such as *Responding to the Needs of Today's Minority Students* (Wright, 1987), a key title in the Jossey-Bass series, New Directions for Student Services. Illustrative of helpful literature available through other publishers is Taylor's (1986) *Effective Ways to Recruit and Retain Minority Students*.

There are also institutional models of success in racial and cultural diversification. This chapter has employed Lynchburg College's experience as an example. The University of Massachusetts–Boston, Miami-Dade Community College, and Mount St. Mary's College are additional models.

The challenge is clear. The appropriate response is equally clear. The resources are available. The only question is whether we as a nation possess the will to change our institutions. If we wish to be on the side of the future, the answer had better be yes.

References

Green, M. *Minorities on Campus: A Handbook for Enhancing Diversity.* Washington, D.C.: American Council on Education, 1989.

Taylor, C. *Effective Ways to Recruit and Retain Minority Students.* Madison, Wisc.: Praxis, 1986.

Wright, D. J. (ed.). *Responding to the Needs of Today's Minority Students.* New Directions for Student Services, no. 38. San Francisco: Jossey-Bass, 1987.

George N. Rainsford is president of Lynchburg College in Virginia.

The essential means of maintaining institutional vitality in our rapidly evolving era is for a college or university to conceive a strategic vision and then to realize that vision through purposefully managed organizational change.

Concluding Observations

Douglas W. Steeples

D. W. Farmer began the first chapter of this volume with the observation that "change always carries with it a sense of violation." That this is so and that as a result individuals, social organizations, and, surely, academic institutions respond to the prospect of change with anxiety, if not outright hostility, is paradoxical. For it is a truism that change is built into the very nature of things. Mark Twain ([1876] 1910), speaking humorously of the amazing variability of New England weather and noting that "in the spring . . . [he] had once counted one hundred and thirty-six different kinds of weather inside of twenty-four hours" (p. 60), might have been prophesying the astonishingly rapid, various, and profound changes that the twentieth century would bring.

New Conditions, New Challenges

The inhabitants of colleges and universities have in the years since 1945 and especially since the early 1970s suffered particularly rude, but not unique, shocks, as their institutions have been thrust from an epoch of luxuriant growth and expansion into an era of instability and competition. Annual classes of high school graduates, traditionally the principal source of new postsecondary students, have in many regions of the country been shrinking for more than a decade and will continue to do so through the turn of the century. An aging national population is further reshaping the academic marketplace. Shifts in public policy priorities have diverted once-abundant government funds to noneducational uses. The rapid growth of racial, ethnic, and other minority groups not formerly regarded as primary consumers of collegiate education is redrawing the national demographic

NEW DIRECTIONS FOR HIGHER EDUCATION, no. 71, Fall 1990 ©Jossey-Bass Inc., Publishers

map. A transforming global economy and political balance announce the advent of an altered world order. Exploding technology and knowledge demand constant adaptation. The notions of reorganization, downsizing, mission and product change, marketing and repositioning in the marketplace, and strategic planning, common in the profit sector, are gaining currency in academia.

Higher education must reply to new circumstances. Colleges and universities must either be changed by external events or attempt to direct their own destinies through purposeful change. As Farmer wrote in Chapter One, "internal and external pressures for change in higher education today make it more realistic for colleges and universities to ask *which* changes they must make, rather than whether or not changes will be required." The problem is to determine which adaptations are necessary or desirable and then to accomplish them. Our task is, in short, to manage change.

The question is: How?

First Considerations

The preceding chapters disclose a cluster of considerations that change agents must address. Among these the most important include the presence of opposition to innovation and the determination of goals and means.

Understanding Resistance to Change. Resistance to change springs from a number of sources. Farmer treated several of these in his chapter on strategies for change. The prospect of doing things differently arouses anxiety in most people, for it promises to replace the sense of security associated with what is familiar with the sense of insecurity associated with what is unfamiliar. Most social institutions are, by nature, conservative. Many if not most professors can be categorized as "hyperconservative." The corporate culture of higher education treasures a body of customary values and practices on our campuses. James Kashner in Chapter Two elaborated on the conserving tendencies of academic culture and on the similar propensities of formally defined institutional hierarchies of role and status. James Pence, considering faculty personnel policy revision, added reference to the habitual regard that faculty members hold for policies that have assumed the status of "sacred texts" and for the opinions of the professorial authors of such texts. Often, these authors command respect as campus "Moses figures." As if these ingredients were not sufficient to discourage all but the most foolhardy proponents of new initiatives, George Rainsford added to them a legacy of racism, usually passive but sometimes active. Then there are the constraints of resources. And one may also cite such factors as sheer inertia and simple contrariness. One familiar definition, celebrating the independence of thought that academics rightly cherish, characterizes a professor as "one who thinks otherwise."

Figuring Out What to Do. Even where it is clear that developments in the external environment or in the circumstances of an institution dictate adaptation, the particular path to be taken is not necessarily obvious. All of the writers who have contributed to this volume assume or state explicitly that specific decisions as to change must rest on a strategic conception. As Farmer put it, "innovations introduced in a college or university should assist in translating its strategic vision into reality. Meaningful change is much more than merely cosmetic; it is tantamount to renewal." Unfortunately, a strategic approach to the direction of higher education institutions is still a relatively unfamiliar phenomenon. There remains a widespread need for the members of our campus communities to learn how to think strategically before they can begin to determine which initiatives are needed.

Steps to Successful Change

Creating a Strategic Vision. The formulation of a strategic vision must precede and inform plans for meaningful innovation—plans that are intended to do more than meet immediate short-term needs. Although strategic planning is not the focus of the present volume, its importance is so critical as to warrant comment here. Keller's (1983) *Academic Strategy* is widely regarded as the best introduction to the subject for higher education. *Successful Strategic Planning* (Steeples, 1988) provides valuable case studies. Both books regard academic strategic thinking and planning as demanding but essential enterprises, each involving many steps and complex processes to forge agreement in several vital areas. These areas include institutional mission, target markets, program priorities, comparative market advantage, and key objectives to be pursued. Strategic planning necessitates constant scanning of the external environment—social, demographic, economic, political, and legal—to identify threats and opportunities. It requires an ongoing survey of an institution's strengths and weaknesses. Above all, it strives to match to best advantage external opportunities with institutional strengths.

Properly undertaken, strategic planning can provide the vision that will show the way for meaningful, purposeful institutional change.

Overcoming Resistance to Change. Several of our writers commented at length on measures essential for creating a campus environment receptive to new initiatives. Kashner showed how change agents must determine whom a projected change might affect and how, as well as who might perceive a desired innovation negatively, who positively. It is also critical to understand which elements of a campus culture will support a project, which will oppose it, and why. The plan to accomplish a desired end should incorporate all of these considerations in evolving a tactic to win support. It must provide for working effectively with sympathetic components of a campus culture and for altering unsympathetic components of the culture as may be needed to allow for approval of intended initiatives.

Kashner, Farmer, and Richard Wood (in Chapter Five) all stressed the importance of furnishing strong administrative leadership, a commitment of resources, monetary and other incentives, and an environment that favors goal setting and rewards the attainment of goals, as means of winning support for change. Provision of data based on research appeals to information-minded faculty members. Use of consultants can also help make a case, as can sending respected faculty members to inspect the working of similar changes on other campuses.

At most institutions of higher education, a broadly participatory process is essential for reaching a decision to innovate significantly. This is especially true where cost cutting and other forms of resource redirection affecting educational offerings are at issue. The experience of Ohio Wesleyan University that Keith Mathews recounted is an important case in point. Program and other initiatives at Westminster and Lynchburg colleges, related to efforts to tap new student markets, also depended heavily on winning needed faculty support. Administrators seeking support are well advised, finally, to heed Wood's caution: "Do not fight unnecessary [political] battles." They need, instead, to hold to a clear sense of priorities, remembering to avoid skirmishes over minor issues that can lead to a defeat over the major goal.

Attempts to change the educational program in the direction of greater coherence face special difficulties. Any such centripetal ventures must overcome the most powerful influences presently at work in this realm, which are centrifugal. The continuing knowledge explosion accelerates disciplinary specialization. Specialization, in turn, encourages the onrushing fragmentation of the academic community and the establishment of new academic units, new boundaries, new pieces of turf. But even here, as Wood showed, determined and entrepreneurial leadership that nourishes creativity and experimentation can win progress.

Providing Leadership. It turns out that managing change in colleges and universities is, at bottom, a matter of judicious administrative leadership. This leadership works steadily to gain allies, frame plans, and work toward approval of projected initiatives. Presidential leadership figures centrally in framing a strategic vision and setting the agenda for innovation. The exercise of administrative leadership has been likened to gardening, with the campus chief executive acting as the gardener in charge. But leaders need to use Wood's "beyond-the-watering-can model." Rather than simply watering every plant in the garden, change agents must water and fertilize selectively, nurturing desirable plants, pruning where necessary, and weeding. Selective gardening must be the rule as long as claims on resources outstrip the available supply.

Implementing Change Effectively. Gaining agreement that innovation is necessary and winning approval for desired initiatives are only the beginning. Change agents must—whether concerned with mission, marketing goals, educational programs, projects to attract new support, institutional reorganization, or some other aspect of a campus—deploy personnel and other resources, employ goal setting and rewards for accomplishment, and use institutional policies and administrative apparatus so as to implement what has been decided on. They must assign responsibility for managing what has been installed, ensuring that results are monitored and that fine-tuning and adjustments occur as needed.

Putting comprehensive organizational change into effect typically means operationalizing it all the way to the level of individual academic units and faculty members. No strategic plan is fully implemented until the departments and other units comprising a college or university have all developed their own lists of objectives to assist in achieving the goals of the institution. King's College used project teams to forward the creation of an outcomes-based, assessment-oriented curriculum. It used growth plans to connect the work of individual professors to institutional aims. Ultimately, the whole faculty joined in revising the content and syllabi of the entire curriculum. Ohio Wesleyan's full faculty provided information used to frame proposals for program reductions and voted on the resulting proposals. Earlham's Quaker heritage dictated reaching decisions by consensus, ensuring extensive participation in prolonged deliberations about virtually all major issues as well as widely decentralized means of implementation. Helmut Hofmann's argument assumed that the activities of all staff members concerned should be related to specified fund-raising goals. At the University of Southern Colorado, the revised faculty handbook directed that professorial performance be measured against the criteria of teaching, scholarly and creative activity, and service. The task of determining what constituted superior, meritorious, and unacceptable levels of effort was left to the school and colleges and to the academic departments. Professors were charged to develop annual growth plans to serve as the basis for measurement. Westminster's enrollment activities require campuswide organization and cooperation.

Once a new system is in place, it is also necessary to recognize successful effort. For example, there might be a public celebration of the work of those who produced a new faculty handbook. A new building might be named for the benefactor whose generosity enabled its construction. Professorial accomplishment might earn a promotion in rank, tenure, or some other suitable award.

Finally, administrators must be prepared when things do not work out as intended, to use Pence's phrase, "to do it over."

Heeding Cautions. Richard Wood offered sage advice to campus officers working to innovate. He reminded us that initiatives will generally take more time than has been anticipated. They will need faculty leadership that will not materialize without administrative leadership and support. They will cost money. They will not progress steadily along the expected path. They will come to fruition only if there is a good flow of communication. There is another caution to add: No change, no matter how fundamental or broad or well conceived, will bring a campus to a final state of perfection or equilibrium with the environment. Given that circumstances will always change, there will be an ongoing need to adapt, innovate, transform, and renew. The need for meaningful institutional change is continuous and permanent. Meeting that need will require great resilience of spirit, creativity, flexibility, capacity for judgment, and tolerance for ambiguity.

Change and Institutional Vitality

There is a story that not long ago a person now directing a major corporate productivity and quality department spoke to a gathering of executives about the dynamics of change and its management. The speaker described a typical cycle of change. The cycle ordinarily begins when an organization feels discomfort. Discomfort prompts new behaviors that in time become habits. If all works as intended, a condition of comfort returns. Discomfort provokes action, but innovation carries the risk of anxiety and further discomfort until the period of transition has been successfully negotiated. The Chinese written character for "crisis" offers a convenient shorthand way of thinking about organizational change. The top element of the character, by itself, signifies "danger," the bottom, "hidden opportunity." The art is to manage affairs so as to minimize the danger and maximize the opportunity. The fact that the cycle of organizational change originates in the perception of a problem is crucial.

At a small university recently, a faculty committee convened to hear a range of proposals designed to combat problems of eroding enrollment, excess capacity, insufficient revenues, and overgrown expenditures. After an hour or so, a frustrated professor blurted, "We wouldn't be talking about these things if we had 200 more students." That is part of the point. Difficulty brings pressure to change, even though the prospect may be unwelcome. The other part of the point is this: Unless an institution remains attuned to evolving external conditions and to its own state, it may slide into crisis. Drift and a complacent stagnation place a campus in jeopardy. The key to vitality is to conceive a strategic vision, then to manage purposeful efforts to realize the vision. There is no greater imperative in higher education today.

References

Keller, G. *Academic Strategy: The Management Revolution in Higher Education.* Baltimore, Md.: Johns Hopkins University Press, 1983.

Steeples, D. W. *Successful Strategic Planning: Case Studies.* New Directions for Higher Education, no. 64. San Francisco: Jossey-Bass, 1988.

Twain, M. "The Weather." In *Mark Twain's Speeches.* New York: Harper & Row, 1910. [Originally delivered 1876.]

Douglas W. Steeples is vice-president for academic affairs at Aurora University, Aurora, Illinois.

INDEX

ORDERING INFORMATION

NEW DIRECTIONS FOR HIGHER EDUCATION is a series of paperback books that provides timely information and authoritative advice about major issues and administrative problems confronting every institution. Books in the series are published quarterly in Fall, Winter, Spring, and Summer and are available for purchase by subscription as well as by single copy.

SUBSCRIPTIONS for 1990 cost $48.00 for individuals (a savings of 20 percent over single-copy prices) and $64.00 for institutions, agencies, and libraries. Please do not send institutional checks for personal subscriptions. Standing orders are accepted.

SINGLE COPIES cost $14.95 when payment accompanies order. (California, New Jersey, New York, and Washington, D.C., residents please include appropriate sales tax.) Billed orders will be charged postage and handling.

DISCOUNTS FOR QUANTITY ORDERS are available. Please write to the address below for information.

ALL ORDERS must include either the name of an individual or an official purchase order number. Please submit your order as follows:
    Subscriptions: specify series and year subscription is to begin
    Single copies: include individual title code (such as HE1)

MAIL ALL ORDERS TO:
    Jossey-Bass Inc., Publishers
    350 Sansome Street
    San Francisco, California 94104

OTHER TITLES AVAILABLE IN THE
NEW DIRECTIONS FOR HIGHER EDUCATION SERIES
Martin Kramer, Editor-in-Chief